Break of Noon

Paul Claudel

Break of Noon

Partage de midi

Edited by Anthony Rudolf

*with essays by David Furlong,
John Naughton and Susannah York*

*Translated by Jonathan Griffin, David Furlong,
John Naughton and Susannah York*

Produced by Exchange Theatre
for the Finborough Theatre

Shearsman Books & Menard Press

First published in the United Kingdom in 2021 by
Shearsman Books Ltd   &   Menard Press
PO Box 4239   8 The Oaks
Swindon   Woodside Avenue
SN3 9FN   London N12 8AR

Shearsman Books Ltd Registered Office
30–31 St. James Place, Mangotsfield, Bristol BS16 9JB
(this address not for correspondence)

www.shearsman.com

ISBN 978-1-84861-755-1

Copyright in Antbony Rudolf's *Preface* and editorial matter
© 2021 Anthony Rudolf
Copyright in John Naughton's essay © 2021 John Naughton
Copyright in David Furlong's essay © 2021 David Furlong
Copyright in Susannah York's essay
© 2021 Estate of Susannah York and Menard Press
Copyright in Jonathan Griffin's contribution
© 2021 Anthony Rudolf, the Jonathan Griffin Estate and Menard Press

Copyright permission to publish this English-language edition
of *Partage de midi*: © 1982, Éditions Gallimard, Paris

Copyright in cover illustration © 2021 Julia Farrer

Contents

Anthony Rudolf: *Preface* / 7

David Furlong: *The Exchange Theatre and Claudel* / 9

John Naughton: *Paul Claudel:* Partage de midi / 15

Paul Claudel: *Break of Noon*

Act I / 29
Act II / 65
Act III / 87

Alternate Ending / 113

Susannah York: *Afterword* / 121

Biographical Notes / 125

Preface

I will not seek to say more about the three essays included here other than to remark that collectively they shed light on the history of the making of this remarkable and complex play and on the history of the efforts to translate it. In a sense, they mirror Paul Claudel's various versions. The three authors, David Furlong, director and translator, Susannah York, actress and translator, John Naughton, professor of French literature who has worked on Claudel for many years, create between themselves a three-way conversation (four-way if we include Jonathan Griffin) about this strange and compelling work.

I have edited this book as part of my ongoing role as Jonathan Griffin's literary executor. It is thirty years since he died and nearly fifty years since Pierre Rouve's Ipswich production of Jonathan's translation, starring Ben Kingsley and Annie Firbank. I believe that Jonathan's famous generosity of spirit would have enabled him to smile at Susannah York's characteristically chirpy and mischievous account of their regular working sessions as co-translators. Her essay, published here as an Afterword, is reprinted in slightly edited form from the version that appears in *Sage Eye* (Menard Press, 1992), a volume of tributes to Griffin I put together after he died. I write shortly after the tenth anniversary of Susannah's death, which was on January 15, 2011.

Observing David Furlong and Fanny Dulin of Exchange Theatre and their equally young team of actors at work during performances of several plays has been an eye-opener for me. John Naughton has been a comrade from the Yves Bonnefoy circle for decades. Furlong, Naughton and York are robust and challenging, as Claudel would have expected. As a fellow translator of Yves Bonnefoy, it is particularly interesting for me to read Naughton's remarks about an earlier French writer than Bonnefoy, who had mixed feelings about Claudel, disapproving of his "idéalisme négatif" but approving of his celebration of terrestrial reality and his recognition of the sacred as incarnated in art.

Yves Bonnefoy would have been intrigued by this book, as I hope its eventual readers – whether in French studies or English theatre or both – will be.

Anthony Rudolf,
London, 3 March, 2021

P.S. My postscript to Susannah's Afterword contains an account of the production of the play she starred in at the French Institute, London and at the Manchester Royal Exchange Theatre in 1991.

The Exchange Theatre and Claudel

David Furlong

In 2006 I directed my first play in London, in English. It was Paul Claudel's *L'échange* (*The Exchange*), and it gave its name to the company I founded with Fanny Dulin, Exchange Theatre.

Paul Claudel was almost completely unknown in the UK, but I thought he could be presented to the London theatre world as "the French T.S. Eliot". The three nights of this first show attracted about 120 people ... Fanny had put her savings into the show, and on top of hiring Jermyn Street Theatre in the heart of the West End, we created a surprisingly bulky set, with costumes by French designer Agnès B. We were absolute beginners. The Claudel play contained the seeds of my future directorial practice, as well as mistakes of logic and beginner's luck... We found the American version by a retired professor, Louise Witherell, from the University of Wisconsin. She was very open and delighted that there was interest in her old 1960s translation.

Claudel's symbolism (and probably mine via the way I directed it) was very well-received by the only reviewer, Michael Donley, who attended on behalf of the Paul Claudel Society: *To tell the truth, we didn't get the impression that it was a "translation", as the dialogues were so fluid, easy, idiomatic. (...) Thomas Pollock Nageoire was the big surprise. A black man, he used musical and rhythmic speech (....) An ingenious transposition of Claudelian musicality (...) We laughed a lot, but the complexity survived. The original direction of David Furlong offered to the British public an approachable Claudel, without betraying the poet. (...) While reading the play again after this production, I saw it in a new light. A good sign, it seems to me. Let's hope there will be a 'reprise', a longer run, later on.*"

There was no longer run. But as we had managed to fill an auditorium for three nights with an almost unknown foreign playwright, I was approached by Neil McPherson from The Finborough Theatre, who was genuinely drawn by the idea of producing a Claudel play. The following month I had my first meeting with Neil, but apart from *The Exchange*, we did not have another Claudel on the horizon. My cast at the time and some anachronistic directorial choices did not fit Finborough's production criteria. So Neil suggested that *The Exchange* was not the show for them, but immediately asked me if another Claudel play might be suitable. I suggested intuitively *Partage de midi*, based on a few things I had read, and a vague memory… but mostly it was a gut feeling.

I immediately re-read the play and it confirmed my instinct that it could be a 'colonial period piece' and I made a wish that one day I would do it. Unconsciously, it allowed me to deepen what I had started doing with *The Exchange*: by changing one of Claudel's main characters from a dominant white male to an empowered black lead actor, I had changed the gaze of the audience while still being absolutely true to Claudel's universalist ideal of the "reunification of the world". This was Michael Donley's "big surprise". I was decolonising my thinking about theatre, and *Partage de midi* immediately contributed to this, as the play deals with some of the actual events of Chinese colonisation.

Exchange Theatre went on to produce 22 shows in 11 years. In 2017, I was nominated for Best Director at the Off West-End awards, and the Finborough attended our acclaimed Molière production. The conversation with Neil was re-ignited. We wanted to collaborate after so many years, and he mentioned that it was the 150th anniversary of Claudel's birth. It was the right time to bring our project to life.

* * *

In 1900, Paul Claudel, then a young 32-year-old diplomat, had an affair with a married woman, named Rosalie Vetch, while he was French consul in China. This love affair had a huge impact on him, and he wrote *Partage de midi*, a semi-autobiographical play, as a catharsis. Because he was both a devout Catholic, and a diplomat representing France abroad, he was warned by his confessor at the time not to publish his play, nor reveal any part of the true story. So, from the moment he finished writing *Partage de midi* in 1905, Claudel immediately banned it from being published or staged. (He did publish a private, limited edition of the work in 1906 for distribution only to close friends and to people he trusted.) He'd already had several of his plays published but this one was to remain generally secret for 42 years – until his friend Jean-Louis Barrault made him change his mind in 1948. By this time, Claudel had become a member of the Académie Française, and he was such an important figure as a diplomat that he'd even been on the cover of *Time* magazine when French ambassador in the USA. After his retirement, his plays were successfully produced year after year in France. Barrault had done some of the productions, especially the epic *Soulier de Satin*. They had talked about *Partage de midi*, and Barrault convinced Claudel to allow him to produce the play. Claudel agreed but revisited the play and completely rewrote the end. From then on, there were two versions of the play.

Fast-forward 70 years. We learned of a translation by Wallace Fowlie and ordered it. We discovered that it was based on the 1948 version. I hoped that I could find a translation of the 1906 version. We then discovered that Jonathan Griffin had made one for the Ipswich Arts Centre in 1972. But how could we get hold of the text? In the British Library archive catalogue, we found a programme – we learned that the cast included the young Ben Kingsley – but no translation.

A week later, I discovered that Griffin was also a respected translator of Portuguese poetry. I found the name of his publisher: Anthony Rudolf of Menard Press, who responded with great enthusiasm. He told us that he had a copy of Jonathan's translation and that as Griffin's literary executor and rights holder he was eager for us to revive it and that he would send it straightaway!

However, once again, it was the 1948 version! To study these translations, we needed the original version. So we ordered the new edition of Claudel's plays, published by La Pléiade in 2011. It turned out that the two versions were not that different, apart from the ending. This was the main change: the 1906 version involved a young man still mourning his love – the one I wanted to direct – whilst the 1948 version was more ironic and less idealistic.

One day at the office, as I was printing out a scanned copy for my assistant director, Anne-Christelle Zanzen, we were discussing Chinese colonialism, the insurrections, and the world of the play. I gave her the script, and when she looked it over, she said "Are there only 35 pages?" In disbelief, I at first thought that she had miscounted... And then I checked Anthony's envelope. I only had Act 1. I called him and he told me that he had sent me everything he had. "This is a catastrophe", he said. Meanwhile, the Finborough, understandably, was showing concerns about the script situation.

It was then that Anthony mentioned to us that in the 1980s, his friend, the actress Susannah York, had fallen in love with the 1906 version and had gone through pretty much the same ordeal to find a translation. She even convinced Jonathan Griffin at the time to let her write a '1906 version' of his translation, which she proceeded to do. It was read at the French Institute in 1991. We needed to find that version. Fortunately, Anthony thought of someone I hadn't called yet: Richard Jackson, who was a close friend of Susannah's, the producer of several plays she directed, and the man who had facilitated the 1991 event. Richard was very welcoming and said he had an audio recording of the 1991 French Institute reading and invited me to collect it. We had the most amazing conversation about his legacy: how he had arranged tours of the Renault-Barrault company in London in the sixties and seventies, how he had produced some Marguerite Duras for the stage, and how he had an ongoing partnership with the French Institute. I mentioned that we used to be resident there, and how strange it was that this place, because they have a team that changes every three years, seems to have permanent amnesia about what great initiatives took place within their walls. The people in posts today don't know about our two years of residency five years ago, so how could anyone remember Richard's work from fifty years ago! After two hours I had to leave and promised to continue the conversation when I returned the tape after transcribing the second and third acts.

By the end of her translation, Susannah York had taken huge liberties in comparison to the French. I ended up having to re-translate, whilst already in rehearsal. I had already done some revision on *The Exchange* and had also adapted Sartre and Molière, so I figured I could do the end of Act 3 myself.

* * *

"Why this woman? Why this woman suddenly on this boat?" (Mesa – *Partage de midi / Break of Noon*).

Claudel said of her, "She was the only woman I passionately loved, the one who played in my life the entire role a woman could play". But the fact is that Rosalie left Claudel in 1904 and made no sign of life until 1917. It was through the resumption of their relationship, eventually on a purely spiritual level, that she revealed to Claudel the reason for her escape: she felt that her rival was none other than God Himself and that she could not replace Him.

I decided to edit down the end of the play to the essence of its symbolism and purity: I wanted to underline most of all the central theme of the divine and eternal dimension of Love and Consent. This is the version we presented at the Finborough Theatre in May 2018. I was finishing assembling the script whilst the actors were already in rehearsals on Act 2. It was quite an accomplishment, at the last minute. I owe a tremendous debt of gratitude to Anthony Rudolf for offering and undertaking to find a publisher for this work, which has now been updated and expanded, and to John Naughton for bringing us his expertise and for translating the two alternate endings.

* * *

When casting and directing the play a few ideas governed my approach in line with the concept of decolonising theatre: I wanted to change the origin of Mesa, the protagonist representing Claudel. As a young diplomat, he had been so immersed in Asian culture that I felt strongly that the part should be played by an actor of Asian descent. I also wanted the ethnicity of Francis Vetch, Rosalie's husband, to be respected in our casting of De Ciz. Finally, I wanted to tell the truth of the woman, Ysé, on whom Rosalie is based. Despite the three male characters around her, the play was never about the male gaze but about her undying power.

BREAK OF NOON was originally presented by Exchange Theatre in association with Neil McPherson at the Finborough Theatre in June 2018.

CAST

Ysé	Elizabeth Boag
Mesa	Matt Lim
De Ciz	David Durham
Amalric	Connor Williams

CREATIVE TEAM

Director	David Furlong
Producer	Fanny Dulin
Costume designer	Sarah Habib
Set Designer	Ninon Fandre
Lighting and Sound Designer	Alastair Borland
Fight director	Lula Suassuna
Assistant Director	Anne-Christelle Zanzen

EXCHANGE THEATRE

Led by David Furlong, artistic director, and Fanny Dulin, producer, Exchange Theatre is an international company established in 2006 in London in order to translate and produce unknown or rare international plays in English. The company has translated Georges Feydeau, Jean-Paul Sartre, Molière, Xavier Durringer for British premieres and developed ambitious productions with a strong visual imagery, original music and multimedia creations. Exchange Theatre was resident company at the Institut Français du Royaume Uni and invested bilingual interactive performances for families and young audience. The company has also investigated bilingual devised works with bicultural casts and creatives exploring under-represented identities. They received Off West-End nominations for best director, best productions and best video design on Molière's *The Doctor in Spite of Himself* and *Misanthrope*.

FINBOROUGH THEATRE

The Finborough Theatre is a fifty-seat theatre in the West Brompton area of London under artistic directorship of Neil McPherson. The theatre presents new British writing, as well as UK and world premieres of new plays primarily from the English-speaking world including North America, Canada, Ireland, and Scotland alongside rarely seen rediscovered 19th and 20th century plays. The venue also presents new and rediscovered music theatre.

Paul Claudel: *Partage de midi*

John Naughton

I

Partage de midi is the most openly and painfully personal and autobiographical of Paul Claudel's many plays. Published privately in 1906 in a limited edition of 150 copies destined for close friends and associates, the play would not see an edition for the general public, nor would it be performed on stage until 1948. For this public exposure to occur, Claudel will have had to confront the resistance of the woman who played such a decisive role in his life and in the play that dramatizes that role, and he will have had to receive the authorization of his Catholic confessors.

It is undeniable that the play registers what in 1908 Claudel himself called "an exact accounting of the horrible adventure where I almost left my soul and my life after ten years of an absolutely chaste and Christian life."[1] The play deals with a painfully conflicted adulterous love affair and is set in China where Claudel occupied a consular post. Although the play is primarily focused on a personal and passionate drama, it also presents a critical perspective on the European colonialists bent on making their fortunes at the expense of the indigenous Chinese population. And as we shall see, for however autobiographical the play may be, the real-life protagonists will undergo transformations that allow them to be integrated into a mythic vision of sin and redemption.

In an essay called 'Romantic Religion', the Jewish theologian Leo Baeck seeks to establish a distinction between Judaism and Christianity by seeing the former as a "classic" religion, the latter as a "romantic" religion.[2] In using the term "romantic," Baeck is borrowing from Schlegel who defined romantic texts as ones that treat sentimental material in a fantastic way. The fundamental content of a romantic orientation are feelings and emotions pushed to an extreme. Its goal is a world where

---

[1] Letter to Louis Massignon, cited in the Preface to *Partage de midi*, edited by Gérald Antoine (Paris: Gallimard, 1994), 7-8.

[2] Leo Baeck, 'Romantic Religion', *Judaism and Christianity*, translated and edited by Walter Kaufmann (Philadelphia, PA: Jewish Publication Society of America, 1958), pp. 189-292.

the extraordinary, the miraculous have the last word. For the romantic, suffering and sorrow are good and valuable as long as the soul can be immersed in them. With the romantic, everything is expressed in superlatives, and all of human and earthly reality is lived on the level of ecstasy. The romantic will often consider his emotional experiences, which by their very suddenness seem the proof of irrecusable authenticity, as the most important things in his existence and as situated therefore in the heart of a transcendent plan. To the extent, however, that the romantic will need to dismiss any reality that might call into question the initial rapture, he will live constantly between exaltation and bitterness. We can certainly observe some of this psychology in play in *Partage de midi*. Ysé recognizes Mesa as "extreme, extreme! headstrong, excessive, always goes too far." The play vacillates between the banal realities and ambitions of the colonialists and a deeper drama that expresses itself on the level of ecstatic revelation. One has only to think of the sudden recognition between the lovers in Act One: "Mesa, it is Ysé, it is I" as though they had drunk the magic love philtre of that other great romance, the one of Tristan and Iseult. Many critics have noticed the resemblances between the medieval romance and the modern work. Wouldn't Claudel have thought of Iseult when he gave Ysé her name? But perhaps the more significant comparison to consider is the one that can be made between Wagner's operatic treatment of the story and Claudel's play. Wagner's opera and Claudel's play have an obvious structural similarity: Act One involves the fatal recognition on board a ship; Act Two takes place in the opera in a garden, which Claudel transforms into a cemetery; Act Three registers the wound and death of the hero. But there are significant differences. As a young man Claudel, like so many of his contemporaries, was drawn to Wagner's music. It was a moment in French cultural history when orchestral pieces were played at popular concerts, "discharging torrents of dream, of nostalgia and of unfounded sentimentality on imaginations open to them," and it is at this moment that "the Wagnerian opium had begun its poisonous role."[3] Now these remarks were made by Claudel in 1939 and reflect a detachment from first encounters during which he found in Wagner and Beethoven his "only rays of hope and consolation" at a moment when materialism and naturalism were dominant forces, and when Darwin, Spencer, Renan, and Taine were masters. For the young Claudel, Wagner evoked the memory of God, of

---

[3] Paul Claudel, «Francis Jammes» in *Œuvres en prose*, ed. Jacques Petit and Charles Galpérine (Paris: Gallimard, Bibliothèque de la Pléiade, 1965), p. 553.

a lost paradise, and of the true life. But with the passing years, a plainly visible detoxification will take place. By 1938, Claudel will say of the forces in play in Wagner's *Tristan*: "I once admired this, today I find it idiotic."[4] And it is in particular the resolution of the opera that Claudel found detestable. More than once, he will rail against the "braying of that great ass, Tristan"[5] in the third act. Claudel cannot accept the welcoming of nothingness and unconsciousness exalted at the end of the opera. Of Wagner's many operas, it is *Tannhäuser* Claudel admires most, since the opera is marked by such clear dualisms, especially between *terrestres* and *célestes*, between carnal love and transcendent love. For Claudel, drama means tension, the conflict of forces in opposition, and it is certainly tension and conflict that we feel in *Partage de midi*. The lovers themselves seem locked in a kind of battle for ascendancy. Mesa gets the final word in the first version of the play when he sees himself in the very last words of the work as "the great male in the glory of God/Man in the splendour of August/Victorious spirit in the transfiguration of Noon". But this "victory" will not be accomplished without formidable struggle and division. I would like first, however, to establish the biographical facts that underlie the literary composition.

II

As a young diplomat assigned to a consular post in China, Claudel will become intimately involved with a beautiful woman of Polish/Scottish origins, named Rosalie Agnès Theresa Ścibor-Rylska, who was born in 1871 in Krakow. The affair is adulterous, since Rosalie is a married woman. Her husband is an unethical schemer, named Francis Vetch, a man bent on making a fortune in China by any means. Rosalie has had six children by Francis Vetch, two of whom have died at birth. Claudel will have met Francis Vetch as early as 1899. It is less clear whether or not he met Rosalie as well at that date. What is certain is that Claudel will reconnect with Francis Vetch, together with his wife and their children, in 1900 on board the steam ship *Ernest-Simons* on a return trip to China after a critical moment spent in France. During this period in France,

---

[4] Paul Claudel, *Journal II 1933–1955*, ed. François Varillon and Jacques Petit (Paris: Gallimard, Bibliothèque de la Pléiade, 1969), p. 227.

[5] *Correspondance Paul Claudel–Jacques Rivière, 1907–1924*, Cahiers Paul Claudel 12, ed. Auguste Anglès and Pierre de Gaulmyn (Paris: Gallimard, 1984), p. 216.

Claudel will seriously consider a vocation to the monastic life, and as an oblate at the Abbey Saint Martin in Ligugé, he will spend time in deep reflection on the possibility of pursuing this life until hearing while at prayer what he believes to be a categorical refusal. Years later, Claudel will remember this rejection as "rien de positif, simplement: *non. Pas autre chose.*"[6] He will live this sense of refusal with bitterness and disorientation. "I had in me the strength of a great hope," Mesa will say in the first act of *Partage de midi*, "and it's gone."

> I have got to return to the same place. Nothing accomplished.
> And here I am, sent back naked, with the old life,
> Dried out, with no other instruction
>   But the old life to be started again, o God!
> Life cut off from life,
> My God, waiting for nothing but
> You alone who want none of me,
>   With a heart wounded, with a strength crippled!

It is in this state of mind that Claudel will return to his post as vice-consul in Fuzhou, China. And in the endless days on board the *Ernest-Simons* he will be side by side with a beautiful and very alluring woman, in the constant proximity of her "face and her warmth".[7] The Vetch couple will wind up with Claudel in Fuzhou, and Francis Vetch will depend on Claudel for assistance as he tries to find ways of advancing his fortunes. Claudel will in fact lodge the couple, together with their children, in his official residence, and the affair with Rosalie will be facilitated by the numerous absences of her husband. The situation is sufficiently scandalous as to cause alarm in the diplomatic hierarchy. The affair will last for the better part of four years, but Rosalie will leave Fuzhou, pregnant with Paul Claudel's child, on August 1st, 1904, never to return. She will take two of her children with her and leave two behind. What is most astonishing is that somewhere on her travels back to Europe, she will meet a Dutch merchant, named John W. Lintner, and agree to live with and be protected by him. Within no time, there is no response from her, and most of Claudel's own letters will be returned unopened.

---

[6] Paul Claudel, *Mémoires improvises*, recueillis par Jean Amrouche (Paris: Gallimard, 2001), 171.

[7] Letter cited in Paul Claudel, *Théâtre I*, ed. Didier Alexandre and Michel Autrand (Paris: Gallimard, Bibliothèque de la Pléiade, 2011), p, 1561.

It is in a state of complete anguish and despair that Claudel will learn of "the horrible betrayal" from one of Rosalie's aunts. He will pursue Rosalie in the company of her husband! to find that she has settled with Lintner in Brussels. Lintner will write to the Quai d'Orsay in Paris to denounce Claudel's behaviour with regard to the Vetch family, offering to submit, if necessary, Claudel's private correspondence with Rosalie and the "injurious" letters he has been writing to her. He asks formally for protection for Rosalie and her children, adding to his petition the unwanted and inappropriate advances of the husband from whom Rosalie is seeking a divorce. Claudel will return to France in acute misery and distress, soon seeking the support of close friends and religious advisers. He will also begin the therapeutic exercise of writing first drafts of the play that will become *Partage de midi*.

The first complete version, distributed privately, certainly registers the excesses of emotion that Leo Baeck identifies as a function of a religious temperament of the romantic sort. In the second act, Mesa professes his love for Ysé in the following way:

> And here I am at the end of my strength like a starving man unable to
> Hold back his tears at the sight of food.
> Oh column! Oh power of my beloved! It's ungodly. It's unjust. I should meet you!
> What should I call you? A mother, because that's a fine thing to have.
> And a sister? I'm holding you, this round feminine arm between my hands.
> And a prey, the smoke of your life comes up through my nostrils, and I'm trembling feeling you weaker like a yielding quarry I have by the neck!

And Claudel will have Ysé say:

> I am Ysé, your soul!
> And what are others to us? You are unique and I am unique.
> And I hear your voice in my entrails like a cry that cannot be endured.
> And I raise myself toward you like an enormous, desiring,
> Dumbfounded creature.
> And what we desire isn't to create but to destroy and ha!
> It's not happiness I bring but your death and mine with it.
> And what care I if I cause you to die
> And me, and everything, and so what, so long as at that price,

Which is you, me, given, thrown, ripped, lacerated, consumed,
I feel your soul, in a moment that is all eternity, touch my soul.

Claudel's first readers were immensely moved by this exalted rhetoric. André Gide wrote enthusiastically and seemingly without irony: "On certain pages of your play, I feel that trembling of Moses before the burning bush..."[8] And André Suarès was equally enthralled: "What a dazzling confession!....You appear in total nakedness. It's not a play and it's more than a play. I feel I'm at some magnificent requiem mass. Mesa's Canticle is worthy of Dante, of the Bible." Suarès perceptively notes the presence of a fifth character, who, though invisible, is omnipresent. "At the hour of noon that seems shadowless, the shadow of God is everywhere: He is the hero of the tragedy."[9] Readers over many generations have shared these feelings and have an unshaken preference for this first version of the play.

III

The real-life drama does not end here, however, since after thirteen years of silence, Rosalie will write to Claudel while he is serving as the French Minister in Brazil, and their relationship will enter a new phase. Though Claudel is now a married man with children, he will reconnect with Rosalie in 1920, and their physical intimacy will resume briefly, before stopping altogether in 1921 when Claudel is made French Ambassador to Japan. It is from this moment forward that Claudel envisions a relationship on a purely spiritual level where his hope is for a peaceful union in heaven. "The joy we were not able to have in this world," he writes to her as early as 1920, "we've put on reserve for eternity."[10] And in 1921, he will add "how beautiful it would be to be able to sleep together..., buried spiritually in each other's arms, in a deep peacefulness, everything between us atoned for and forgiven."[11] This period of reconnection and mutual examination of the turbulent events of 1900–1904 will lead to

---

[8] *Paul Claudel et André Gide: Correspondance 1899–1926*, Preface and Notes by Robert Mallet (Paris: Gallimard, 1949), p. 67.

[9] *André Suarès et Paul Claudel: Correspondance 1904–1938*, Preface and Notes by Robert Mallet (Paris: Gallimard, 1951), p. 89.

[10] Letter cited in Paul Claudel, *Partage de midi*, ed. by Gérald Antoine (Paris: Gallimard/Folio, 1994), p. 256.

[11] Op cit, p. 257.

a time of emotional appeasement in Claudel, a better understanding of Rosalie's actions in 1904, and to a sense of gratitude toward her for leaving him, something he acknowledges he would have been incapable of doing himself. Claudel now views her decision to leave him as heroic, and as inspired by God. Increasingly, he will come to see the passion he felt for her as an experience of love that allowed the rigid and egotistical man he had become to understand the reality of someone other than himself. In his great canticle in the last act of the play, Mesa will exclaim,

> And because I was an egotist, this is how you punish me
> By the dreadful love of another!

Rosalie will continue to inspire a great deal of Claudel's writing, in particular his renowned epic drama, *The Satin Slipper*, published in 1929 and staged in 1943, where her redemptive role is underscored.

The truth, however, is that with the years that pass, the person called Rosalie Vetch, who exists in real time and space, will become an increasing disappointment and burden for Paul Claudel. To his credit, he will provide support for her and their daughter Louise until Rosalie's death in 1951, and he will ensure continuing care for Louise until her death in 1996. He will in fact use his influence to help the careers of Rosalie's children by Francis Vetch, and his generosity will extend even to assistance for Rosalie's child by John W. Lintner, his rival. Reading the many years of Claudel's correspondence with Rosalie[12], one is painfully aware of the gradual ebbing of rapturous devotion, surely brought on in part by the endless requests for financial support. Already in a letter of 1921, Claudel seems aware that he has very little in common with the woman he otherwise associates with the physical incarnation of his own soul. "You say we are alike, and it's true, but how different we are as well, especially in religious matters." And he continues in a disturbingly misogynist vein, "At bottom, I think that the majority of women don't have much religious feeling…. Their lovers, their children, and for most women, the clothes they wear, are the primary and sole interests of existence."[13] The person to whom he will refer as "my beloved, my

---

[12] See Paul Claudel, *Lettres à Ysé*, ed. Gérald Antoine, Préface Jacques Julliard, (Paris: Gallimard, 2017).

[13] *Op cit*, p. 146. Claudel's remark reminds one of a similar observation made by Baudelaire in one of his "intimate notebooks": "I've always been amazed that women are allowed to go into churches. What conversation could they

angel, the star of my life whom I will love forever"[14] in 1921 will be addressed more distantly in much later letters and without the passionate salutations and valedictions of an earlier time. What a painful evolution for Claudel to have outlived his ecstatic dream and to have finished in an attitude of bitterness and indifference toward the one who was once his great love and source of poetic inspiration! This imposition of real life upon exalted artistic recreation explains in part the efforts Claudel made in his revisions of the play for the production of 1948 to diminish some of the high-flying rhetoric and to cast Mesa more clearly as narrow-minded, self-centred, and small and Ysé as the woman chosen by God, but "drawn by lots," to correct and chasten that egotism.

IV

The title of Claudel's play, *Partage de midi*, is meant to underscore a crucial turning point. The four main characters are in the middle of their lives, at its decisive juncture. The catholic Mesa, in particular, realizes that, like Dante, he is "*nel mezzo del cammin*". They all can feel that they have arrived at "Noon: at the centre of [their] lives". They are together at this moment "cut off from the earth" with nothing but water behind and before them. Ysé, it should be noted, is an orphan. "I didn't have parents to raise me," she says in the first act, "I'm a foreigner, I don't use every word as I should." Like the others, she is constantly on the move "without having been able to settle anywhere." Claudel has commented on the meaning of the names he has assigned to his characters. They each, he feels, represent some idea of *middle* or break. Ysé in Greek means equal. Mesa means half. The syllables in Amalric's name divide into three separate syllables. De Ciz evokes cutting, as the French word for scissors is *ciseaux*.

In the earliest manuscript version of the play, Claudel had originally imagined three main characters: Mesa, the husband called Legrand, and Ysé who are dramatized in only the first two acts. Amalric is present in the second manuscript version, and he is an all-important addition because he allows Claudel to create a third act. The character Amalric may be based in part on a fellow companion on the *Ernest-Simons*, a loquacious

---

have with God?" Charles Baudelaire, «Mon cœur mis à nu» in *Journaux intimes* in *Œuvres complètes*, ed. Claude Pichois (Paris: Gallimard, Bibliothèque de la Pléiade, 1975), p. 693.

[14] *Lettres à Ysé*, p.204.

and jovial personage, named Marie-Auguste Castanier, but by the second manuscript version of the play, Claudel is aware of the presence of John W. Lintner in Rosalie Vetch's life and may even have caught a glimpse of him in Brussels. Amalric becomes the rival in *Partage de midi*, and he will do battle with Mesa for control of Ysé.

If the first two acts of the play are based quite closely on real life events, the same cannot be said of the third act. In the 1906 version of the play, Claudel creates an imaginary reconnection between Mesa and Ysé and the consecration of a marriage between them that will persist beyond death. Claudel composes this resolution having lost all contact with the real life Ysé, Rosalie Vetch. The ending is therefore a purely phantasmic conjecture. By 1948, Claudel will have long reestablished a relationship with Rosalie and have pursued it in an increasingly diminished form until shortly before her death. For the version of 1948, Claudel benefits not only from perspectives and explanations given by Rosalie, especially during the 1920s, but also from the vantage point provided by more than forty years of distance from the events that gave rise to the first version of the play. In the 1948 version of the play, the lovers see each other as instruments provided by God to inspire them toward heaven. They will have understood that their love for one another, if absolutized, will lead only to frustration, but because of this recognition, they will learn to redirect their love to its true object which is God.

What is especially striking about the third act, in all of its versions, is the way in which the act is placed in the background of an insurrection in China. The Boxer Rebellion (1899–1901) was a recent memory that the consul Paul Claudel would have been painfully aware of. It marked the resistance of some Chinese in the North to the foreign, imperialist presence in China, especially in the form of Christian missionaries. (During the period in 1900 when he is considering monastic life, Claudel's spiritual counsellors at Ligugé advised him to remember his duties in China at such a grave and critical moment.) Throughout the play, Claudel will underscore and expose the racist, exploitative nature of the colonialists. In Act Three, Ysé is with Amalric as the two prepare for death. Rather than succumbing to the approaching insurrectionists, they have decided to blow themselves up in their house to avoid capture. Ysé lives in terror of "all those yellow bodies all together like a cake swarming with maggots… you'd say they don't have real blood." Despite the fact that *Partage de midi* concerns itself with a private and passionate love affair, its cultural setting is never far from sight. Mesa feels disdain for the colonialists he associates with: "And us, the whites," he says, "gossips, cynics, in petticoats and trousers, drinkers without thirst, pig eaters!" They are presented as uniformly and basely acquisitive. "We must all get rich! Or if not, it's our own fault. I mean to make a pile and a half!" says Amalric, who adds "we're like tigers among weaker animals."

> Obviously instead of this wretched commerce,
> It would be better to enter sword in hand, terribly,
> Into the old cities melting with human flesh,
> Resolved to return with – for one's own share – four barrels
> brim full of jewels, and here and there
> a few infidels' ears and fingers chopped from matrons
> and young maidens,
> Or perish with honour in the midst of one's companions!

Future productions of this play will have ample opportunity to bring out this background and to explore the degree to which the impossible and disastrous love affair is a function of its historical and cultural setting.

V

The present translation, the work of many hands and brought together by David Furlong, is based in part on the revisions Claudel made for the staging of the play in 1948 as well as on the first version of 1906, itself the product of many reworkings by Claudel. The first version, the one François Mauriac said was for "les connaisseurs de Dieu," has an intensity missing in the later revisions, and this is because, as I have said, Claudel was understanding the experience that gave rise to the play in a new way, and from the perspective of being so many years removed from it. But it should also be noted that the first version has often proved difficult to perform in English translation, critics finding the language somewhat stilted and laboriously "metaphysical". "More poem than play," Susannah York has remarked, "a glorious metaphysical piece rich in characterization and *vie intérieure* but untheatrical...."[15]

---

[15] Susannah York, 'For Jonathan, without whom' in *Sage Eye: The Aesthetic Passion of Jonathan Griffin*, ed. Anthony Rudolf (London: The Menard Press/King's College, 1992), p. 97, and reprinted slightly revised as the afterword to the present volume.

Through the various versions of this play, we can measure the degree to which Claudel is obsessed with the events of 1900-1904 and perceive his ongoing effort to better understand the moments that would structure so much of his future life. The relationship between Ysé and Mesa could easily be viewed as a banal bourgeois drama elevated to the level of mystical passion by an overexcited and deeply romantic religious imagination, but the revisions to the play also allow us to see the poet in dialogue with that imagination.

With this in mind, we thought it would be useful for the reader to compare the way in which the play ends in the 1906 version to the way it ends in the much later revised text. We used the text Claudel published in 1949, which contains revisions to the version created for the production of the play in 1948. We have placed this 1949 revised text as an appendix after the version based largely on the 1906 text. There are many cuts in our translation(s), and some minor liberties have been taken with the French, but these English renderings have been put together with an eye to future productions of the play on English stages.

John Naughton

Break of Noon

Characters:

Ysé
Mesa
Amalric
De Ciz

ACT I

The deck of a large stream ship somewhere in the Indian Ocean heading toward the Far East.

AMALRIC	My friend, you've let him tie you up in knots.
MESA	It's not done yet.
AMALRIC	Then don't do it. Trust me. I like you, Mesa: Don't do it.
MESA	It doesn't seem to me such a bad deal.
AMALRIC	But the man who's making it?
MESA	Well, he has his qualities.
AMALRIC	I hate weak people and it scares me. Just you do it. Just you go in with that fancy fellow! And there you'll be, like a man with an overflowing seltzer bottle, and nowhere to put it down. I hear he's going to move in with you, bag and baggage. Bag and baggage, including the wife. I'm warning you, Mesa. And what do you make of her, the wife? Here they are.

Ysé and De Ciz appear on the deck coming up from the first class.

YSÉ	Noon.
DE CIZ	We will soon reach a viewpoint.

Boat horn.

MESA	What a cry in the desert of fire!
DE CIZ	Sh! Look!

Opening the awning.

YSÉ	God of our fathers! Don't open the awning!
AMALRIC	Blinding. Like a gun flash! That's not a sun anymore!

De Ciz It's lightning! How reduced and consumed one feels, in this blast furnace!

Amalric Each thing is horribly visible, like a flea between two glass plates.

Mesa How fine it is! How hard!
The sea, with her resplendent spine,
Is like a stunned cow being branded with the red-hot iron.
And he, you know, her lover they call him, the one whose sculpture you see in the museums,
Baal,
This time he's not her lover, he's the executioner sacrificing her! Those are not kisses, it's the knife in her entrails!
And face to face she returns him blow for blow.
No form, no colour, pure, enormous, fulminating.

Ysé How hot it is! How many days more to the Minnicoi light?

Mesa I remember that little night-light on the waters.

De Ciz Do you know how many more days, Amalric?

Amalric God, no! And how many days already since we left? I've forgotten.

Mesa The days are so alike, they make only one single huge day, white and black.

Amalric I adore this huge, motionless day. I'm at my ease. I adore this huge hour without shadow.
I exist, I see.
I am not sweating. I'm smoking my cigar. I am satisfied.

Ysé Listen to him, satisfied! And you, Mesa?
Are you satisfied? Me, I'm not satisfied!

DE CIZ	She's crazy.
You'd better see about our luggage. The whole ship's in confusion because of the party this evening.
MESA	The party? Marvellous! That gives us the whole day with the ship to ourselves. I'm in favour.
DE CIZ	My dear, I need your help, really I do.
YSÉ	I run! I fly! I must see to my children.
And you two, don't you stir from here! I'm coming back, I forbid you to stir.

They both exit.

AMALRIC	There. Is she not charming?
MESA	You know very well I know nothing about women.
AMALRIC	That, I'm sure is true. And women will never know anything of you.
I like you, and I know you. Better than you think! – She's in love with me, that is a fact.
And yet you attract her, it's funny, she's frightened of you! And she always wants to know what you think of her. That's vexing for me, don't you think?
MESA	I think she's a shameless coquette.
AMALRIC	You make me laugh with your "shameless coquette". You're off the mark.
My dear man, she's a superb woman.
MESA	That's what you've never stopped ramming down my throat since we left Marseille.
AMALRIC	But it's true. And you still don't see it! Well, well! Miles away as you are, I do believe I've got that into your head, just a little at last!

The scene you made yesterday evening! And that cigarette she gave you,

You who don't smoke, how devotedly you finished it! Come on, don't be coy!

MESA   You're being stupid.

AMALRIC   My dear man, say what you like, I only go for blondes. She's not a coquette, you watch out! She's a warrior, she's a conqueror!

She has to subjugate and tyrannise, or give herself

Clumsily like a great beast!

She's a thoroughbred, and it would amuse me to mount her, if I had time.

But she is riderless, with all those foals following her about,

She runs free like a naked horse.

I see her shying, smashing everything, smashing herself up.

She's a foreigner among us.

She's out of her place and not in her breed.

She's a wife for a chief; she should have had great duties to bind her, a great gold horse-cloth,

But that husband of hers,

That fancy fellow, that thin Provençal with the soft eyes, a sort of dud engineer and wheeler-dealer.

You can see that for her he's a vice. All he's managed is to get her with children.

It's frightening to see them all on their way to China!

They will not leave you. Be careful with them, my young friend!

– Here they are.

Ysé re-enters followed by De Ciz carrying her luggage.

YSÉ   *Laughing, after looking at each of them one by one.*

Me, I'm not satisfied !

(Pointing at Mesa.) And here's another one who's unsatisfied. *(Pointing at De Ciz.)* And another who's unsatisfied.

It bothers him, fetching and carrying for me! The gentleman is not content.

Why is he not content? He always looks as if he's pretending to smile. But I am content. But I am contented, like it or not!

She laughs out loud.

MESA You are content and Amalric is satisfied.

DE CIZ Because he's successful.

AMALRIC Me? I was cleaned out last year.
Rinsed like a beer-glass! Heigh-ho! I'm starting again.

MESA Contented, because he is needed.

AMALRIC Because he is busy, quite simply!
A lot of things that I need, A lot of things that need me.

YSÉ Amalric, you will be successful. You know how to use your hands. What you do you do well.
I like a person who can use his hands.

MESA He has pleasing hands. (Because life is like a cow
And she knows all about not getting milked unless she wishes.)

DE CIZ He's well sprung. He's assured of his place everywhere, no matter where!

YSÉ And I have no place anywhere. A deck chair tied to a piece of luggage, a bunch of keys in my hand bag.
For the last ten years, that has been my household and my hearth!

MESA *Pointing at the sun.*
Hearth? There is our hearth, straying flock that we are! Alight and drawing splendidly isn't it?

	Suits us well, after all!
Look at him, the master up there, with a thousand million rays busied over the earth
Like an old woman over the chains of the crochet.
Ysé	He's too busy! He's killing me! Give us a bit of hope that night will come!
Amalric	The full force of the sun, the full force of my life.
It's good to be able to look everything in the face, death as well, and I have the strength to stand up to it.
Mesa	Noon in the sky. Noon at the centre of our life.
The same for each of us, and here we are gathered round it, at the very middle of the whole horizon, free, stripped,
Untied from land, looking behind and before.
Ysé	Behind… All that enormous past behind us, pushing us with an irresistible power, And before us that enormous future drawing us in with an irresistible power.
De Ciz	How bitter it is to have finished being young!
Mesa	Formidable, to be beginning to finish being alive!
Amalric	And glorious to be not dead, but alive.
Ysé	The morning was more beautiful.
Mesa	The evening will be more so.
Did you see, yesterday
All that was being born from the great substance of the sea?
Foliage masses, green,
And lakes, rose and tobacco, and streaks of red fire in the teaming bright chaos
The colour, oily, the colour of all the colours of the world.
The sea, the profound window!

You'll see all that when they raise the awnings. There's the evening: never stops coming and comes all the same.

AMALRIC   I always say
The best hour is this. I ask for one thing only, that's all: to see clear,
To see well,
Things as they are, not as I want them; what I have to do.

DE CIZ   There's no more time to lose.

MESA   It is not time that's short, it is we who fall short of time.

AMALRIC   Take what comes, all of you! Just let my chance come by, I shan't miss it.

YSÉ   How odd it is, all the same!
The birds and the little fishes
Have a place to make their home, a hedgerow, a hole under the willow stump.
But the four of us have not been able to settle anywhere.
Here we are, gently rocking, on this travelling ship, in the middle of an absurd sea!
You others are free! But I, poor woman with an apron full of children, each with four limbs, and that means mouths as well!
And now, I must manage to live like a boy with these three men who never leave my side! And my home
Is these eight pieces of luggage on the bill of landing,
Three cabin trunks, three trunks and two cases, in the hold, a suitcase and a hat-box. My poor hats!

MESA   This is the age when to be free is no longer all that reassuring.

AMALRIC   No gloomy foreboding. Let's study our faces as one does at poker, when the cards are dealt: It's important before you even look at your own hand.

> Here we are in the game engaged like four needles, and who knows what
> Destiny has ready for us four to knit together?

De Ciz There's no more time to lose. No time to pick and choose. Mesa, another word with you, please!

De Ciz and Mesa exit.

Ysé So you didn't know we were aboard?

Amalric We were already out at sea when I recognised you. That tall woman setting her shoulder to the wind!

Ysé You recognised me at once? I've not changed so much in the last ten years?

Amalric The same, so very much your own self.
Even more perfectly the same than before!

Ysé Imagine! Someone told me you were dead!

Amalric What an idea! Me? Die? Not on my life?

Ysé I was sure we would meet again.

Amalric One look was enough.
The same woman I knew. Same gait.
Same back suddenly against the air. Free and straight. Bold, supple, resolute.

Ysé Still pretty?

Pause.

Amalric I knew you all right.

Ysé I remember! I had on my long cloak and my felt hat.

Amalric "It's her!" It was you.

Ysé	I was happy!
After all, deep down, one's always happy
To leave, to leave the whole lot behind.
Hmm? Not a hat, not a handkerchief waved to us!
Amalric	No.
Ysé	Not some poor little woman somewhere snivelling her heart out?
Some widow, kindness itself, some young virgin as straight as a reed and rounded like a whistle.

She laughs.

All right. All right. It doesn't matter.
– I was happy!
How salty it all was! One of those wicked ravaged skies,
That I love. And the sea, how she leapt at us, the pagan! That was a sea!
But this, here,
This is a floor one skates on, boringly. And so perfectly polished it's embarrassing.
What a magnificent mess
We are making on it! But you say you like these sleeping, sleep-bringing waters.

Amalric I like them. I like the feel of us drilling our hole through them and going straight on.
And I hate being handled, tossed, dandled, scrubbed, thrashed, tumbled without rhyme or reason,
Like up there off Crete, oh, my God, d'you remember! By the maniac of a wind.
Here it's all finished for good, and a good thing too! All *resolved* for good.
The situation
Reduced to its primal features, as in the days of the creation:
The Waters, the Heaven, and me between them like the hero Izdubar.

Ysé	Amalric! You did not always have such a hatred
For that maniac of a wind without rhyme or reason.

Silence.

Amalric	Ysé, why wouldn't you, then?
Ysé	You had no money.
Amalric	And what else?
Ysé	You seemed too strong to me, too self-assured,
Exasperating! Too sure of yourself. Rather ridiculous the faith you have in yourself, a kind of religious faith!
I want a person to have need of me! You see people can do without you.
Amalric	And what else?
Ysé	And
I felt weak when you were near. That annoyed me.
Amalric	And that's why you married him?
Ysé	I love him. I did love him.
Amalric	Lady, of you two, he's not the stronger!
Ysé	When he looks at me in a certain way, I feel ashamed.
When he looks at me with those wide eyes with their long lashes (He has a woman's eyes)
With his great black eyes (in which you can't see a thing)
My heart turns over, ah, before long I've let him do what he wants. I've tried, resist him I cannot.
Amalric	And that's why you are angry with him. Yet he loves you.
Ysé	He doesn't love me!
He loves me in his way. He loves only himself. I remember our wedding night.

And all those children I had, one after another! Because there was one I lost.

The escapes, the panics, the adventures! All the crises with creditors! It's a joke, if you only knew! So many years of my youth gone!

AMALRIC   And yet, Ysé, Ysé, Ysé,

That great flashing morning when we met! Ysé, that cold flashing Sunday at ten o'clock on the sea!

What a wild wind, blowing in the full sun! How it whistled and slashed, and how the steel mistral harrowed the broken water!

The whole sea raised up upon itself, slapping, stamping, kicking at the sun, bolting in the storm-wind!

Only that night by moonlight, in the deepest part of the night

Having entered the straits of Sicilia, those who were waking, sitting up, wiping the steam from the porthole,

Had at last found Europe again, covered in snow, huge and grey,

Voiceless, faceless, welcoming them in sleep.

And now this bright day of epiphany, we were leaving behind us on our right,

Corsica, white, radiant, like a bride in the bell-filled morning!

Ysé, you were returning from Egypt then, and I, I was surfacing again from the far end of the world, from the ends of the sea,

Having drunk down my first great gulp of life and carrying back in my pocket

Nothing but a hard fist and fingers that had learned to count.

A gust of wind like a slap

Exploded all your combs, and flung in my face the pile of your hair!

Look at the tall young girl

Who turns, laughing; she looks at me and I at her.

YSÉ   I remember! You were letting your beard grow, it was stiff as a curry-comb!

How strong and joyous I was then!
And how pretty I was too!
And then life came, the children came,
And now you see me subdued and obedient
Like an old white horse who follows the hand that pulls him,
Counting his four feet one after another!

She laughs out loud.

AMALRIC Well! I see you can still laugh!

YSÉ I've been held in prison, and now I'm free and the sea air is going to my head!
– Amalric, you shouldn't have been so quick to believe me, you shouldn't have taken me so cruelly at my word,
I was mad then! It's funny! I feel such a little girl still!
Look, I had no parents to bring me up, Amalric. A foreigner, I don't use the right words.
I've grown alone, in my own way, you mustn't judge me harshly.
With another man it might have been different.

AMALRIC Those fine shining eyes! And now there are tears! You poor little lamb.

They both laugh.

YSÉ And here I am, setting off again, where, I've no idea.

AMALRIC What? Hasn't your husband affairs waiting for him in China?

YSÉ Nothing at all, only his luck in which he trusts.

AMALRIC Bah! He's a rubber plant always ready to take and to flourish! He's a gluttonous creeper! He'll find his tree, the right tree.
I've noticed he's talking a lot
With our companion, Mesa.

Pause.

	Mesa
	Has spoken to me about the railway they are building
	Toward Siam, the telegraph lines to the Shan States,
	you know? The Shan States mean nothing to you?

Ysé I don't know a thing. Heigh Ho! We always have landed on our feet.

Amalric Mesa. I like chatting with him. He never looks at you.
Instead of looking at you straight,
It's as though he were looking at you somewhere else,
in a mirror. He's listening to you, somewhere, as he reasons.
You see each of his thoughts as it comes. It's pitiable!
He's rough, stiff and rough, like those who have within them:
"A great sowing to defend"
I think he's a virgin.

Ysé Don't make fun of him!

Amalric I? I'm not making fun of him. Look, you're angry. I like him. Don't be cross.

Ysé I respect the fellow and would like him to like me and respect me!
Why are you always with me and never leave my side?
What must people think? I saw him just now looking at us
And I'm sure he saw us yesterday
When you kissed me.

Amalric I'll leave you in peace.

Ysé Seeing him alone, I went over to him the other night,
You know, when we invited that poor chap over,
Leonard, who was singing his poor, silly cafe song.
He'd wandered off.

You remember? I was wearing my black dress crêpe-de-chine
You think it suits me.
And I came looking for him and leaned on the rail beside him, and he really insulted me with all his heart,
Treating me as,
As treated I've never been!
I adore that! Holy smoke! As you say! And I was asking forgiveness and weeping hot tears like a little girl!

AMALRIC   Poor Ysé!

YSÉ   Yes, you're right, Poor Ysé! Ysé! Ysé, poor, poor Ysé!

AMALRIC   Poor Mesa!

YSÉ   They say he has a great position in China.

AMALRIC   He was made head of the customs when quite young. He speaks all the dialects. He's advisor to the Viceroys of the south.
He's the one with the most influence in those parts.
He's a gloomy creature, he's tired, he has "other ideas". He says that he's going back there for the last time. Religious mania. Holy smoke. Religious mania is the word for it.
This deal your husband's discussing with him, I don't know what it is
Appeals to him. I told him to watch out. He's looking
For someone for his cables. It's big business.
Very big business. The climate – to say that the climate is good, good, good,
Honestly would not be true. But your husband
Is used to these hot countries, isn't he?

YSÉ   Anything to do with electricity has always interested him.

AMALRIC   How lucky! So, we'll leave them to sort it out between them, him and Mesa,
And I will leave, taking Ysé, holding Ysé, carrying Ysé with me, where I go.

YSÉ   Really ?
You think I'm there for the taking, you think I can be carried off, just like that?

AMALRIC   And yet, suppose I wanted to !
When I do want to, my Amazon, I shall lay my hand on your shoulder,
I shall take Ysé, I shall hold Ysé, I shall carry Ysé off,
With this hand here, with this hand which you see, which is a big coarse hand.

YSÉ   Too bad for you then. I don't bring happiness where I go.

AMALRIC   Ysé, it's true, why wait?
I have pleasing hands.
You know very well that you won't find
The strength you need with anyone but me, and that I am the man.

YSÉ   The man! He says he is the man! And I – am I perhaps not the woman? What do you say to that? Leave me.

He looks at her thoughtfully. She keeps her eyes on her book. He takes a cigar and goes off. Mesa comes in and moves awkwardly toward Ysé, and seeing she is not looking at him, he remains hesitant.

MESA   What are you reading there that's worn-out and dog-eared like a love story?

YSÉ   A love-story.

MESA   Page 250. You were right to skip the outer pages.
The difficult part is the ending, it's always the same thing,
Death or the midwife. You have to read in both directions at once.

YSÉ   It's always too long. Anything written about love ought to be as sudden
As a flower, for instance, a scent, and you're sure of having had it all, of having it all,

45

> Of drawing it all in at one go, it made you say "Ah!" simply;
> A scent so direct, so prompt, that it made you simply
> Smile, a little: "ah!" and there you've gone on!

MESA It isn't a flower one sniffs at.

YSÉ Love, you mean? I was talking of a book.
But love itself,
Well, what about it?
I would really like to know what that is.

MESA Well! So would I! Silly, the things you make me say! All the same, I can understand…

YSÉ Un – der – stand! Listen to him! My poor man, you don't have to understand! You have to lose consciousness. I'm too bad, I can't!
It's an operation to submit to! It's the wad of ether they shove under your nose.
Adam's sleep, you know? It's in the bible. That's how the first woman was made.
A woman, think for a moment, all the beings that are in me. She has to let it happen!
She has to die
In the arms of the man who loves her. And has she any idea, poor innocent
None at all! What there is in her and what is going to come out of her? She knows nothing! Nothing of nothing, of nothing at all! A mother of women and men!

MESA What is there to ask of a woman?

YSÉ Many things it seems to me. Among others, this child she didn't ask for!

MESA Children ? What on earth next? You've misunderstood what I was trying to say the other day!
I imagine it's such a wound,
Such a commotion of one's substance…

He stutters, hesitates, closes his mouth, his eyes shining.
She laughs out loud.

Ysé Talk professor, I'm listening! No need to get angry!

Mesa It's all there is,
Simply all in him asking for all in another, in a woman!
That is what I was trying to say. Laugh if you like.
Laughing stupidly won't help!
  A child indeed! It's the man himself to be born,
Into an eternal moment.
  But all love is only a sort of shoddy comedy badly acted
  Between the man and the woman; the questions are not put. That's what I was trying to say, the questions are not put.

Ysé The comedy is amusing, sometimes.

Mesa Perhaps. I have no sense of humour.

Ysé And yet you talk better than my book
When you want to! How your eyes shine, professor,
When you're made to talk
  Philosophy! You have fine grey eyes. I like watching you seethe! I like
  Hearing you talk, even when I don't understand.
  Be my teacher!
  Don't shy away! I'm uneducated, I'm stupid!
  Don't judge me harshly, I'm not as bad as you imagine. I just don't think.
  No-one has taught me. No-one ever talked to me as you did, the other evening.
  I know you're right, I'm bad.

Mesa It's not for me to judge you.

Pause.

Ysé Stay, don't go.

Mesa I don't want to go.

Ysé	And then, one never knows what you're thinking!
So here we are, the two of us. You and me, how sad that is!
There is between us such a suspense, a state of exclusion so fine
That the least little thought disturbs it!
Poor Mesa! I see you so unhappy! Mesa! Don't think I'm full of joy.
Mesa	I'm not unhappy.
Ysé	You must take care of yourself. They told me you now don't eat. Why look so fierce?
Mesa	Who "told you"? I am not unhappy. I've nothing to say to you!
Go and gossip with Amalric! You're not playing the mother, you're not playing the coquette with me!
If I feel sadness, I've a right to it. Some grief – it's my own! That at least is my own!
That at least is my own.
Ysé	Don't be cruel.
Mesa	You'd like to make me talk. Be honest, it would amuse you to have me make calf's eyes!
You know so well how those poor devils, those boys,
Love nothing so much as talking, lying, displaying their noble heart,
How I've suffered, O God, if you knew! How handsome I am!
I've nothing to say to you! You are happy, are you not? That is enough.
Ysé	Are you sure that I'm happy?
Mesa	You must be. You ought to be.
Ysé	Ah? Well, if I cling to that happiness or whatever it is you call that.

	May I be a different woman! Shame on me if I am not ready to shake it from my head Like an arrangement of hair which I undo.
MESA	Keep the dreadful stuff tied up! Laughing? Blushing? Don't deny that you're happy!
YSÉ	Don't reproach me.
MESA	I like looking at you. You're beautiful.
YSÉ	You think so really? I'm glad that you find me beautiful.
MESA	How it frightens me to see you like this, So beautiful, so fresh, so young, so wild with that fellow you've found for a husband Knowing as I do the country where you're going!
YSÉ	Amalric said the same thing.

A beat.

Don't desert us!
You know we shall be staying for some time in Hong Kong
Where you live, I think.

Silence.

Well? Does that displease you?

MESA	I'm not coming back to China for long. The time it will take to settle my affairs.
YSÉ	A year, perhaps, two years?
MESA	Yes… Perhaps … More or less.
YSÉ	And then?

Mesa And then nothing!

Ysé A year perhaps, two years, more or less, and then nothing?

Mesa And then nothing! Yes. What is that to you?
 Your life is arranged! I am an outcast you know, one of those yellow pariah dogs, what does my life matter to you? Everyone loves you!

Ysé Does that anger you?

Mesa Live your life, your mess of a life! As for me, I want Nothing. I've left the world of men.

Ysé You're taking the whole lot with you.

Mesa Laugh! You are beautiful and joyful, and I am sinister and alone…
 And I want nothing at all! What could you have to do with me? What is there between you and me?

Pause.

Ysé Mesa, I am Ysé, it is I.

Mesa It's too late.
 All is finished. Why have you come in search of me?

Ysé Have I not found you?

Mesa All is finished, I tell you! I was not expecting you.
 I had so carefully arranged
 To withdraw, to go out from among men, well! Yes, from among men!
 It was done, why do you come in search of me? Why do you come to disturb me?

Ysé That is what women are made for.

MESA	I was wrong, I was wrong.
To chat and… let myself be tamed like this with you, Trustingly, as by some charming child whose beautiful face one loves looking at, and the child is a woman, it's stupid, one laughs when she laughs!
What have I to do with you? What have you to do with me?
I tell you, everything is over.
It's you! But not more you than any other woman!
What is there to expect? What is there to understand in a woman?
What has she to give you, after all? And what she asks of you!
One would have to give oneself entirely to her!
And there's absolutely no way, and what would be the good?
There is no way of giving you my soul, Ysé.
That is why I turned in a different direction.
And now why do you come disturbing me? Why do you come to seek me out? That is cruel.
Why have I met you? And here, now, attending to me.
You turn towards me your enchanting face. It's too late!
You know very well that it's impossible! And I know you don't love me.
For one thing, you're married, and for another I know you're attracted to
That other man, Amalric.
But why is it that I say that, and what is it to me?
Do as you please. Soon we shall be separated. What I have at least is mine. What I have at least is mine!
YSÉ	What do you fear in me, since I am the impossible. So?
Raise your eyes and look at me who am looking at you with my face that is impossible.
MESA	I know I don't attract you.
YSÉ	It's not that at all, but I don't understand you.
Who you are, who it is you want, who it is one has to be, how

| | I am to deal with you, you are strange.
| | Don't make a face, it's ugly! Yes, I think you are right, you are not
| | A man who would be made for a woman
| | And in whom she would feel well and sure.

MESA | That is true. I have to stay alone.

YSÉ | It would be better that we arrive and not be together anymore.

Pause.

MESA | Why?
| | Why is this happening? And why must I meet you
| | On this ship, at this instant when my strength has diminished, because of my blood that has flowed?
| | – Do you believe in God?

YSÉ | I don't know. I've never thought about it.

MESA | But you believe in yourself and that you are beautiful
| | With a profound conviction.

YSÉ | If I'm beautiful, it's not my fault.

MESA | You, at least – one at least knows who you are and with whom one is dealing,
| | But imagine someone with you
| | Forever. In oneself, and having to tolerate in yourself another.
| | He lives, I live. He thinks and I weigh in my heart his thought.
| | He who made my eyes may I never see him? Of him who made my heart
| | I can never rid myself. You don't understand me? But it's not to do with understanding!
| | Can a word understand itself?
| | For that there must be someone who'll read it.

| | It's to do with eyes which merely by looking at you, render you comprehensible.
Oh, the torment of feeling oneself studied, spelt out as though by someone who's never satisfied! He gives me no rest!
I fled to the extremity of the earth,
Far from the old house in the straw like a broken egg –
I who so loved those visible things. Oh, I had so much to ask them, and they so much to tell me!
To know all, in order to be all known.
There was someone who would seek me out there, too! And I am like a debtor who is being pressed to pay and has no idea what he owes. |
|---|---|
| Ysé | And so you went back to France? |
| Mesa | What could I do? Where is my fault?
Is it fair
This restraint to pay a debt one knows nothing of?
Well, here I am, help yourself! Take what you want! |
| Ysé | You were rejected? |
| Mesa | I was not rejected. I merely found myself, so it seemed,
Before someone who looks and says nothing. Not a word…
Things are not going well in China. I've been sent back here for a time. |
| Ysé | Bear the time. |
| Mesa | And what else have I been doing these last five years? I have lived in such solitude among men!
I have not come to terms with them at all!
I don't serve.
I've nothing to give to or receive from anyone.
Well, then, let the Silent Partner take back his investment! I ask nothing better than to give it back. "No…"
I left. I have got to return to the same place. Nothing accomplished. I had in me |

The strength of a great hope. It's gone. And here I am, sent back naked, with the old life;
Dried out with no instructions but the old life to take up again, o God! Life, cut off from life,
My God, waiting for you alone who want nothing of me, with a heart wounded. With a strength crippled!
And here I am chatting to you! How, I'd like to know, can all this regard you or interest you?

Ysé I am looking at you, it does regard me,
And I see your thoughts rise confusedly to your lips and to your eyes, like sparrows near a haystack, when one claps one's hands all together.

Mesa You don't understand me.

Ysé I understand that you're unhappy.

Mesa That at least is my own.

Ysé Isn't it? Wouldn't it be better if Ysé were your own?

Pause.

Mesa *Heavily.*
That is impossible

Ysé Of course it is impossible

Mesa Let me look at you, since you are forbidden.
Why are you looking at me like that?

Ysé Poor Mesa! It's odd! I've never seen you before.
I like each one of your features, but of course no-one would think of finding you handsome.
Perhaps because you're not tall enough. I don't find you handsome at all.

Mesa Ysé,
Answer me, so I know. Soon we shall be separated.

| | So it can't matter.
| | Suppose
| | Both of us were free, would you consent to marry me?

Ysé   No, no, Mesa.

Mesa   You are Ysé. I know that you are Ysé.

Ysé   It's true. Why did I say that earlier?
          I don't know. I don't know what came over me quite suddenly,
          Something new all of a sudden,
          Something quite new
          Impelled me. The word
          Hardly out, I was shocked. Do you always know what you are saying?

Mesa   I know you do not love me.

Ysé   But that's it, that's what took me by surprise! That's what I discovered all at once!
          I am the woman you would have loved!

Mesa   Let me look at you. How bitter
          It is to have you with me like this! If I stretch out my hand
          I can touch you, and if I speak
          You answer me and hear what I say.

Ysé   I wasn't expecting it! I was not paying attention to you. I respect you. I have not been playing the coquette with you. You can't say that… I don't like to think that.

Mesa   Why is it now that I meet you? Ah, I am made I am made for joy,
          Like a drunken bee in the horn of fertilised flower.
          It is hard, keeping your heart to yourself! It's hard not being loved. It's hard to be alone. It is hard, to wait.
          And endure and wait, and always still waiting!

And here I am at this noon hour when you see so clearly what is right up, so close
That now you can't see anything else. So you are here!
Ah, how the present waits upon us, close at hand.
Like something inevitable.
I have no defences left! My God, I cannot I can't wait anymore!

Ysé No, no, you must not love me. No, Mesa, you must not love me.
That would be not good at all.
You know I'm a wretched woman. Go on being the Mesa I need.
And that great rough man, clumsy and good, clumsy and good, who talked to me the other night.
What will there be for me to respect
And to love, if you are in love with me? No, Mesa, you must not love me.
I merely wanted to chat, to scratch you a little, I thought I was stronger than you
In a way. And now it's I who, like a fool,
Don't know what to say any more, like someone reduced to silence, listening!
You know I'm a poor woman and that if you speak to me in a certain way.
It doesn't have to be loud, but if you call me by my name, by your name,
By a name which you know and I don't
A woman in me listening will not be able to help responding.
And I feel that this woman will not be at all good
For you, but fatal, and for me it means terrible things, I feel it! I don't want to give myself entirely.
And death is not beautiful to me, I'm young,
It's life that looks beautiful! How life has gone to my head on this ship!
That is why all must be ended between us.
It's all said, Mesa. All is finished between us. Let's agree that we will not love each other.
Say you will not love me. Ysé, I shall not love you.

MESA   Ysé, I shall not love you.

YSÉ   Ysé, I shall not love you.

MESA   I shall not love you.

> *They stare at each other.*

YSÉ   *Softly*
                Say it again so that I hear it.

MESA   I shall not love you.

> *Enters Amalric.*

AMALRIC   Sorry, sorry, Monsieur, Madame, forgive my disturbing you.
                Mesa's in demand for tonight's fancy dress ball.
                The singer from Saigon says she can't manage without him. She's in her stays and is showing off her back. Thick velvet! A thick white velvet.
                The only thing prettier was that ox they were flaying yesterday on deck.
                If only you'd seen it! Iridescent, pearly. What there can be under a skin!

YSÉ   Really?

AMALRIC   I'm lying.
                What could you two possibly be talking about? He never leaves your side.
                I don't recognise him. You've changed, little Mesa.

YSÉ   He is moralising. It's refreshing from time to time, to be preached to. He's my professor.

AMALRIC   You are his as well.

YSÉ   There are things to learn from him! He knows about women. That's what he's there for in a way: to advise.

| | One of those men who are always ready to offer their life and who'd give it
If that meant they were rid of you. Extreme, Extreme! Headstrong, excessive,
Always goes too far. Isn't that true? That's what I like about little Mesa.
That's how I am too. |

MESA   Quite true. Being with a woman feels good.
          Like sitting in the shade – and I love hearing her talk very wisely.
          Saying harsh, shrewd,
          Practical, basely true things, the kind that women think of.
          It does me good.

AMALRIC   Things your husband hears?
          He smiles, and one can see he's on the verge of saying something, but he says nothing.
          He's quiet and content.

YSÉ   Poor boy!

AMALRIC   You wouldn't by any chance love him?

YSÉ   I love him! I am the man! I love him as one loves a woman.

She bursts into laughter.

MESA   How can you laugh?

YSÉ   But it suits me, professor! I'm no Frenchwoman.

She laughs.

AMALRIC   Look at his expression when you laugh! It irritates and enchants him.

YSÉ   I like a man who is one man only and has in his back a big hard bone.

AMALRIC   A big hard bone? That's me! The slave and the fireman: that's what most women admire. That's me, both together, slave and fireman!

MESA   I like our own ones, the stokers, when they came up from below, in the evening,
            With only their white teeth to say their prayers in this Arabia of the sea!
            When a man has shovelled all day long in the coal-dust, feeding the yellow sultan,
            With what dignity he can take, soberly, his mug of water!
            And us, the whites – gossips, cynics, in petticoats and trousers, drinkers without thirst, pig-eaters!

AMALRIC   It's true, we don't gain from being herded together.

MESA   The disgust of sitting down at table with all the rest
            Of this herd of hairless animals who stink of cleanliness!

YSÉ   What a difficult man! I find it amusing, it's so nicely adjusted,
            So neat, such fun to watch the whole lot walking, talking,
            Sitting down, turning, thrusting a hand into a trouser pocket. There's plenty to laugh at!
            And a ship, just think, with all its compartments, with all these doors which open and shut,
            What a lovely toy! It's like a naturalist's box full of his harvest.
            All the species together!
            Such fun to watch the way they approach and recognise each other,
            With antennae, sort of picking their way across a face, to observe how they're dressed, combed, shop; the shoes and ties they wear.
            The book they're carrying, their nails, the shape of their ears, the tip of the tongue appearing between the lips like a large almond!
            Just a hand

                    Opening and waving how busy with its delicate fingers!
                    How one understands what it is saying!

MESA   They bore me.

YSÉ   And what do they think of you?

MESA   I don't know. I don't dwell on it. I don't think of other people.

YSÉ   Mesa! Mesa!

MESA   Heavens, it's true : Can it really be true that I think only of myself?

YSÉ   You've just found that out? Now try and pretend that women serve no purpose!
                    You think about yourself and yourself alone.
                    It is easier, Mesa, to offer oneself than to give oneself

MESA   It is true.

YSÉ   Learn one thing about women! A woman is more of a burden than you think!
                    A woman of your own, and you needing her only, all the time, her and no other! She gives herself to you and he, the man, does he give himself to me?

AMALRIC   That's all too subtle for me. Hell! If a man had to spend all his time
                    Finicking over his wife, to find out if he has measured correctly, verifying the state of her heart – what a bore!
                    Emotion is just women's petty cash, like those boxes where they keep a whole lot of ribbons and reels of cotton and buttons of all sorts, and bits of whalebone.
                    And what's horrible is that they're always feeling ill.
                    Anyhow she's there, she's there, isn't she? To be put up with as best you can. There'd be a gap if she wasn't. It's a nice thing to have around from time to time…

What do you say, my boy?
Am I right or not?

YSÉ Amalric… What was it our friend the leather merchant used to say?
"You are a bunny." Amalric, you're a funny bunny.

She bursts into laughter.

AMALRIC And let me tell you, dear lady, don't get too excited over your Mesa!
He's a man who has done too few crooked things in his life.
Here's your husband coming down to us.
Always distinguished and silent, a noble figure!

De Ciz enters.

Ciz, we're all going to get rich!

DE CIZ Amen!

AMALRIC No question at all! In the first place, don't we all need money?
Well, then?
Ask the lady there! Mesa too, who's like a man with no pockets. Not to mention you and me!
I tell you, I smell luck in the air! I'm sniffing it up! I'm filling my kitty full of it! And I should know! I recognise that smell! It hits you in the face!
Ah ! I can feel it, my heart's swelling, we've crossed a certain line! I recognise my old east.
It's India there before us! Can't you hear it? So full,
One can hear the rustle of those hundreds of millions of eyes blinking!
Heh! What luck all the same to be no longer in France! We'll never go backwards again! How dull and watery all that fodder was beginning to seem!
The horror of that wishy-washy greenery! And that was no sun —

	That pathetic bath-water-heater!
DE CIZ	Once again, we've passed Suez.
AMALRIC	We'll never pass it again, hurrah! We shall never go back again, hurrah! But we shall all be dead next year, hurrah!
YSÉ	There's a fine prayer!
AMALRIC	Anyhow, we must all get rich! Or if not, it's our own fault! Now's your chance. I mean to make a pile and a half! I recognise my brave Empire of the Sun! "I'm wild and woolly and full of fleas"! There the sun is sun, I should say! The green is green, and the heat's enough to kill you and hell! When it's red, it's red! We're like tigers among weaker animals! Obviously, instead of this wretched commerce, It would be better to enter sword in hand, terribly, Into the old cities melting with human flesh, Resolved to return with – for one's own share – four barrels brim-full of jewels, with here and there a few infidels ears and fingers chopped from matrons and young maidens Or to perish with honour in the midst of one's companions! That would be better than sweating in pyjamas in front of one's ledger.
YSÉ	And you'll keep the pearls for me!
AMALRIC	Of course! Spare a hope that I find labour for my rubber plantation, and then just see the price I'll get for it! Times change nothing there, always the same sun. Always my Indian, ploughed and sown by the two monsoons, the old scorching pagan! But this country of water – the helmsman knows it's ways well and how it moves! It remains the same thing always. Tell me, do you know where we are? Do you understand the trade conditions? Listen, I'm going to give you a lesson in economics.

Mesa   You're drunk, Amalric!

De Ciz   Never as drunk as he'd like to make you think! He's a true "traveller" watch that eye of his winking.

Amalric   To left, Babylon and the whole bazaar, the rivers descending from Armenia,
    To right, the equator, Africa.
    Well! At once don't you see the trade?
    The great hulks in the North monsoon, scudding from Sheba, streaming from the ports of Solomon,
    Streaming from Muscat and from India, streaming from the mouth of the Two Rivers,
    Laden with iron, laden with textiles, and as many chains and handcuffs as are needed to be enough,
    Bound for Cimbebasia and the Oval Cities!
    And returning before the south monsoon with a pocket full of
    Negroes, negresses, negrilloes, shouting, eating, dancing, chanting, weeping, shitting, pissing!
    And sometimes in the morning the black buttocks of the fat boat, motionless
    In the midst of chicken feathers and banana skins on a sea that spits flying-fish!
    Even there you have all the rubber trade you could ask for!

Ysé   Ah! We've passed Suez for good!

Mesa   We shall never pass it again.

Ysé   The setting sun, the wind is rising…

Mesa   Look at the golden sea.
    "The sea changes colour like the eyes of a woman you hold in your arms"

A bell clangs.

De Ciz   The bell! Time to change for dinner…

Amalric   A woman! Here's a quote I'd never have expected
            Of the Mesa I've come to know. Hehe! He's passed Suez too!
            Mesa! It's our age! It's the age when we should become ourselves!

Mesa   Impossibility of stopping in any place.

De Ciz   Dinner.

Amalric   "The sea like the eyes of a woman who knows! The sea like the eyes of a woman you hold in your arms!"

ACT II

Hong Kong.

The cemetery full of thick trees of Happy Valley. From there, roads can be seen, a racecourse, a factory, a small port, the sea, and beyond, the China coast.

A somber April afternoon. A heavy, stormy sky.

MESA	This is it. *(He reads the inscription on a tomb)*
	I can't be wrong. I can't be wrong. The only neglected Chinese tomb. Leftover from the yellow cemetery upon which the other, the white, has superimposed itself. Tough luck on the first occupants. Each to his turn.
	I wonder what those little lights in the trees are. It must be a Parsee cemetery, I suppose.
	There.
	It has to be said, these Chinese tombs had more dignity. This kind of Omega, like arms reaching out to me, holding me, warming me, cooling me. There's no chance of escape.
	"SMITH"
	You come to toast Mr. Chang Lao Ye and all he can reply is:
	SMITH. Smith! Someone who found no other pretext for living than those five letters: S.M.I.T.H. How original! How worth while to leave Leeds or Birmingham to mingle Smith with the other human pickings the cemetery keeper thought fit to pile up in this little corner to await the broom and the barrow.
	What am I doing talking to myself? The taste of my stomach is in my mouth.
	But she said she'd meet me here.
	No help for it, I've been struck!
	This heart I've started to have, beating instead of a soul, my soul dumping me all of a sudden! Disastrous poisoned sweetness!
	The soul in me like a gold coin between a gambler's fingers. Heads or tails.
	No, not gold, Lead more like.
	I'm going. It'll serve the lady right to find no one here. Yes! I've an idea it'll serve the lady right!

He exits.
Enter De Ciz and Ysé.

DE CIZ	My dear, forgive me. I'm sorry but I must leave you here. I've got a meeting.
	Do not

| | Tell me I can't land on my feet. How many days have we been here? The deal I think is going to run like clockwork.
Let me see it through! You always doubt me.
I've got to speak to my friend Ah Fat. You know that weird Chinese man down there by the port.
I'm having dinner with him this evening to fix the final details.
Then off to Swatow. |

Ysé   It's not dangerous ?

De Ciz   I don't think so. I don't know. Do you think I'm afraid then? It's an honest deal, all in good faith.

Ysé   You pick up languages so quickly!

De Ciz   I know a lot of characters already, I used to collect Chinese seals.

Ysé   I know you're very clever,
Ciz. You could do as well as anyone if you wanted to. Why do you have this passion to behave like a dishonest child?

De Ciz   Dishonest! It's circumstances that are dishonest. You'll see if I'm a child!
No one can see in people, like I can, the desire they didn't know they had to do me a good turn.
These coffins, coolies being repatriated from Penang or Singapore.
If there was opium or guns inside,
I'd be shocked.
Well what do you want my dear? One has to live. An odd occupation for a well-brought up young man. Well what do you think about it all?

Ysé   What do you want me to think? You'd better to keep it to yourself.

DE CIZ	You never know if by baiting the line you catch a little fish. I couldn't risk saying anything to Mesa to arouse his suspicions.
YSÉ	Couldn't you?
DE CIZ	No, it doesn't matter. He's a friend. A real friend. Odd, I really like him.
YSÉ	Let's use him then!
DE CIZ	You're so relentless. I still can't get used to you, This manner you have of insisting and exaggerating and dotting the "i". One needs the light touch in life. Like the children say, "be light". I like the fellow, I'm very happy he can do something for me. And anyway he's got nothing to do with all this.
YSÉ	When do you say you'll be back?
DE CIZ	In a month, fortnight, six weeks, it's hard to be sure.
YSÉ	You're never sure.
DE CIZ	You know we found the best hotel. You get used to hotels. Mesa will keep you company.
YSÉ	Don't go.
DE CIZ	But I must. I'm telling you, I must, I haven't got a penny.
YSÉ	My friend, don't go.

Pause.

DE CIZ	I have to go, I have to, Ysé.
YSÉ	Don't leave me alone here.

De Ciz   There's no danger.

Ysé   You must not leave me alone.

De Ciz   And I'm telling you we must be reasonable.

Ysé   I'm only a woman, I'm afraid.
              Terrible things are lying in wait for me.
              I'm afraid of this stifling country I don't know
              Where you're leaving me alone still dazed and swaying from a ship I hardly left.

De Ciz   What? What do I hear? Can this be Ysé telling me she's frightened?

Ysé   Take me with you!

De Ciz   You can't leave the children.

Ysé   You worry enough about the children but about me not at all, not a bit!

De Ciz   But, Ysé!

Ysé   I implore you not to go and leave me here alone.
              You're always accusing me of being proud, of never wanting to say or do anything, or ask for anything. Well now you see me humbled.
              Don't go. Don't leave me here alone.

De Ciz   So
              She has to confess in the end that she, after all, that she does need, just a little, her funny old thing of a husband.
              Our proud Ysé
              Asking like a child not to be left alone.

Ysé   Don't be too sure of me.

De Ciz   You're mine.
              You wanted to marry me didn't you? Well like it or not

I was the one who took you, who won you, when others failed.

Ysé Don't hold me too cheaply. Don't be so sure of this woman
You hold and caress.
Haven't I been with you for ten years? For ten years I've considered you
From in front, from behind, from in profile, from below and above, and I've arrived at a judgement.
Haven't you had your fill already? Haven't you had all these children with me?
Do you know who I am? A man
Knows no more of his wife than he knows of his mother.
Ten years: My youth is gone, and what I would give is given.
It's done, I've given it all. Don't leave me alone
Because something is done. Don't be away.

De Ciz I know you better than you do.
This proud Ysé! With me! I know you too well to think you would harm me.

Ysé I don't know. I feel temptation in me.
I am no longer the young girl you took.
You haven't been careful with me. I'm not intact.
Do you think I'm only made to have children?
Am I not so beautiful for anything else?
Whoever would have me, I would want him to have nothing else, be entirely his.
There is a certain totality of myself
I haven't surrendered. A certain death
I would know how to give and am I not beautiful? But you, I've understood you are not serious.
Radically not serious.

De Ciz Have I been unkind? Have I ever
Forbidden you anything?

Ysé	Oh would to God you had! That you forbid me myself!

After all I'm a woman, that's not so complicated. What does a woman need

But security, like a honeybee, busy in a clean closed hive?

Not this terrible liberty. Haven't I given myself?
And I long to believe I could be tranquil
At last, safe, that there'd always be someone there
To guide me, a man who'd arrange whatever happened,
To be stronger than me.
And what does it matter if you hurt me, as long as I feel
That you are holding me and I am beholden to you.

But you, who knows you, who can believe you, who can find in you

Something to understand and be devoted to? You flee, you're not there, a weak and tender child,

Capricious, secretive, full of lies and dishonesty and no one can see anything in your eyes.

Forget this going! Don't be absent in the middle of my life!

De Ciz	All this for a few days of absence!
Ysé	Yes.

What if it is the time when a separation is all that is needed?

A knife is a slender thing, but the fruit is cut and can't be rejoined.

Who knows

If I'm not going to die once you're gone? I'm afraid of dying.

Why did you bring me here? Look at this sad place we're in.

It's so hot. And I'm cold.

She looks around her with horror.

De Ciz	But it was you who liked this place and insisted on showing it to me.

Ysé   It is terrible to die. To be dead.

De Ciz   There's no question of dying. Stop talking of that. You must have a temperature? Take some quinine when you get back. There's no danger, I'll be back soon.
Soon we'll have money, a lot of money, and we'll go back to France.
Say what you like. I know you love me. I know it *bonita*!

Ysé   You're set on going?

De Ciz   I must, I have no choice. Ah Fat's advanced me money.

Ysé   Go then. It's alright. There's nothing more to say. Good.

De Ciz   You're not angry with me?

Ysé   No.

Pause.

De Ciz   Ysé, I've been thinking about your advice. There's some truth in it.
These two projects Mesa's offering…

Ysé   Yes?

De Ciz   To stay here, job's not brilliant

Ysé   But it's safe.

De Ciz   Safe, Safe! That's all you can think about!
You've never understood me. I have to be able to use my initiative.
I need to make money.
It's true that money doesn't particularly like me but I like it.
You think I'm scared of a few risks?
It's true, I couldn't take you with me to the Shan state.

YSÉ   That's why you shouldn't go.

DE CIZ   It's a shame. It's only a few years, the position's made for me and I'm made for it

YSÉ   How can anyone agree with you? You change all the time.

DE CIZ   Don't be hard on me. I shan't be here soon. Goodbye, my heart.

YSÉ   Goodbye Ciz. You weren't a bad man.

DE CIZ   No tears, my heart. Goodbye *bonita*.
            I'm not leaving you alone. I'm glad Mesa's here to keep you company.

Ciz leaves. Ysé stares at him leaving. She stays still.

YSÉ   I don't see him anywhere. I'm not going to wait. He might've been kept. So much the better.

*She remains motionless, eyes on the ground.
Mesa comes up behind her.*

MESA   *Softly.*
            It's me.

*She turns slowly toward him and extends her hand.
They look at one another uncomfortably.*

YSÉ   My husband's just left. I couldn't hold him.

MESA   How are you?

YSÉ   Oh. I'm fine. At least I'm still eating.

She bursts out laughing.

Mesa	Have you talked to him?
Ysé	I begged him not to go, not to leave me here alone. But he said no.
Mesa	I've done what I could too. How could he leave you? I've made various propositions. He prefers his manoeuvres, he thinks he's deceiving me. And have you heard all these rumours of revolution?
Ysé	Is something really about to happen?
Mesa	Oh the end of the world is always about to happen. Who really knows China? Two years, maybe three, four more… When did you say he was leaving?
Ysé	Tomorrow.
Mesa	How long will he be away?
Ysé	One month. And you know you must leave me alone. You mustn't come to see me.
Mesa	Of course.

They remain silent without looking at each other. Then suddenly Ysé lifts up her head and opens her arms to Mesa. He clasps her sobbing, his head against her side.

Ysé	Poor Mesa!
Mesa	Ysé !
Ysé	Poor Mesa!
Mesa	It's over.
Ysé	Come! Come and don't stay away from me any longer.

They embrace each other.

Mesa O Ysé.

Ysé Here I am, Mesa, it is I.

Mesa O woman in my arms.

Ysé Do you know what a woman is now?

Mesa I have found you.

Ysé I'm yours.
I'm not leaving you, you can do what you want.

Mesa Oh Ysé! This is a forbidden thing.

Ysé Is it? Look how tight you are holding me! Poor Ysé! I did not think it so forbidden.

Mesa Oh Ysé! The ship that carried us, we saw her sail away, vanish in her own smoke.

Ysé It is not a ship you are holding, but a living woman.

Mesa Ysé, don't let me go back.

Ysé I yield. I am yours.

Mesa She says "I yield. I am yours".

Ysé And you. To me, you must yield to me.

Mesa I'm holding you. To sail away with you. I'm holding you, my great ship!

Ysé Is it enough? Is there more to ask me?

Mesa I have caught you, I am holding your body in my arms and it's not resisting. And I feel this beating heart in my body.

This is it!

It's true, you're only a woman. But I, I am only a man,

And here I am at the end of my strength like a starving man unable to hold back his tears at the sight of food.

Oh column! Oh power of my beloved! It's ungodly, it's unjust, I should meet you!

What should I call you? A mother, because that's a fine thing to have.

And a sister? I'm holding you, this round feminine arm between my hands.

And a prey, the smoke of your life comes up through my nostrils, and I'm trembling feeling you weaker like a yielding quarry I have by the neck.

What is it that's been done to me? What is it that's been placed in my arms like a fallen creature, one who sleeps and knows all, in these misgiving arms.

Tell me presence, tell me power of one who sleeps and knows all,

If you are she whom I love. Oh it was too much in the end and I should not have met you. And so you are mine and you love me, and my heart ceases and dies.

Ysé You're holding me. I'm holding you. My flesh shudders.

I don't draw back, I remain stunned. There she is, then, she who you found so proud and wicked.

You don't know what a woman is, or her ways and how easy it is for her to yield,

To suddenly find herself abject, submissive and waiting,

And heavy and numbed and speechless in the hand of her enemy, incapable of moving a finger.

Oh my Mesa you are no longer simply a man, but mine who am a woman,

And I am the man in you, you are the woman in me, and the same heart beats in us both, we are one using a single heart to be two. We have no names now. There's no more Mesa. And Ysé? There's no more Ysé now. And I mustn't be able to understand. I mustn't be called by names that others know, but by other names so strange like those in dreams that are noiseless, nor by my name, my poor false name. Only as you say it, Ysé, so it can reach only my heart.

MESA   I shall not scold you again Ysé.

YSÉ   True? Are you pleased with me professor? No more scolding?

MESA   Poor teacher that I was.

YSÉ   Tell me Mesa, isn't it better
To no longer feel yourself superior to anyone, but the weakest thing there is,
   A man in the arms of a woman, like a thing on the ground that can fall no more. A simple man, in the end, in my arms.

MESA   Oh I am not a strong man, who said I was a strong man? But I was a man of desires
   Desperately turned towards happiness, desperately turned towards happiness, and tense and loving and deep and undone.
   Who said you are happiness? For you are not happiness, you are what there is in place of happiness.
   I shuddered recognizing you and my whole soul yielded,
   And I love you and I tell you I love you and I hear myself tell you I love you and I can't take it anymore.
   And I wed you in unholy love and damned vows, oh dear creature who is not happiness.

YSÉ   Mesa is simply a man in love.

MESA   A man caught

YSÉ   A man who is mine,
The whole piece under my hand on your shoulder like a stunned beast. And me, am I a man? (*She laughs*)

MESA   Don't be a fool.

YSÉ   Answer me. Am I a man?

MESA   You are a woman

Ysé	And yet I have arms and legs like any other and I can answer when you speak. But a woman is better and more beautiful and kinder.
But tell me the truth, is it true that you have never known another woman?
Mesa	It is true
Ysé:	I am content.
Content to be everything
For you, content to have everything for myself.
But wait, show me your eyes
Which have the colour of mine, and don't hold them elsewhere for even a moment,
Oh I know these devouring eyes, and how long I've waited for them to gaze at me.
Look at me, here I am
Look at each part of me, examine me like a vase newly bought,
That you hold up to the sunlight, see the enamel and this flaw that you trace with your nail,
The maker's brand.
Mesa	You are radiant and splendid! You are beautiful like the young Apollo!
You are as straight as a column! You are clear as the rising sun!
You are as fresh as a rose beneath the dew! Like the dawn and like the green sea in the morning, you rival a great acacia tree in full bloom, like a peacock in paradise.
Ysé	It is fitting that I be beautiful
With this present I bring to you.
Mesa	A priceless thing, truly.
Ysé	A cumbersome thing, Mesa, an enormous thing that is difficult to house,
And which a wise man would not accept in his home.

Mesa I am not a wise man

Ysé It is love, Mesa and I will not call it a good thing. He is a fool that tries to use it
For his own pleasure and thinks the heat good for his home like a well made fire
That will warm the soup or a torch that will melt gold.
Do you know what you are doing Mesa?

Mesa I know only you, Ysé

Ysé I am Ysé, your soul.
And what are others to us? You are unique and I am unique.
And I hear your voice in my entrails like a cry that cannot be endured,
And I raise myself towards you like an enormous, desiring, dumbfounded creature.
And what we desire isn't to create but to destroy and ha!
It's not happiness I bring but your death, and mine with it.
And what care I if I cause you to die,
And me, and everything, and so what, so long as at that price, which is you, me,
Given, thrown, ripped, lacerated, consumed,
I feel your soul, in a moment that is all eternity, touch my soul.
Take mine.
What is it?

Mesa Nothing. I thought I heard someone calling me. Ysé.

Ysé I'm here, Mesa, why are you calling me.

Mesa Ysé, there's no one left in the world.

Ysé There is no one who calls and recalls you now.
I, before you knew me, was here.
Calling you and whom you remember.

Mesa I remember you.

Ysé You remember? Tell me…

Mesa What should I tell you?

Ysé Everything. We have to get to know each other a little, you and I. All your life !
All your life and how it was when I wasn't there, and how it was when I was there but wasn't there with you.
Now I have come. She has come, Ysé. There's no denying it, I am here. And don't think I'm going to let you slip away. That you'll ever slip away between these two fine hands, this right and this left. You'll never slip away so easily when you've taken so long to arrive.
I am she who is forbidden. And what is going to happen? We'll see, what is going to happen.
Look at me, Mesa, for I am she who is forbidden.

Mesa I know

Ysé And am I less desirable or beautiful for that?

Mesa Not less

Ysé Swear it!
And I swear that you are mine and I shall not let you go, and that I am yours,
Yes, in the face of everything, and I shall not cease to be so, come what may. Yes though I be damned,
And I am told to finish loving you!

Mesa Don't say those frightful words.

Ysé Here are other words:
This man, this man called my husband and whom I hate
Is here, and you must send him away,
And should he die, so much better, we will be together.

Mesa That would not be good.

Ysé	Good? And what is good or bad but what prevents or allows our love?
Mesa	I believe that in his heart he himself Wants to go to the place I told him of.
Ysé	Then why should we prevent him? He will ask you to stay But you must not allow it and he will have to do what you want Send him away, somewhere else, where you will, not to be seen or heard again. And let him die if he wishes it! So much the better! I don't know this man anymore! Here he is.

Enter De Ciz.

De Ciz	Hello!
Ysé	Mesa, this is my husband who has come to see you on business. Business which has nothing to do with you. Ciz, this is Mr. Head of the Customs, look at him well. He has his eye on you and is suspicious. You can't throw dust in his eyes, he knows. He bores me. Since you're here, I give you to him. I'm off! I'm going to see my grass cloth, you know, that blue and white one we looked at the other day? Mesa, that address you gave me, the big Cantonese man, Ah Fat – oh no: Not Ah Fat, certainly not Ah Fat! Ah Tung, I mean. Farewell, Ciz.
De Ciz	Farewell.
Ysé	Farewell Mesa. Mesa, you must come and visit me while my husband is away. I am a widow!

Ysé exits.

Mesa How is business, Ciz?

De Ciz Slow. Strange country. Nothing happens as you expect.

Mesa Is it true you know this Ah Fat?

De Ciz I don't.

Mesa So much the better. There's nothing to be gained with the Chinese, you'll find that out.
And I hear you're leaving. Where to?

De Ciz Maybe… tomorrow – I'm not sure. I'm going to Manila.

Mesa Well, I'll see you to the boat.

De Ciz No, don't do that. It leaves very early.

Mesa Have you thought over what I was saying the other day?

De Ciz I've thought about it.

Mesa And what have you decided? I need to know

De Ciz Well, my wife wants me to do it. I can't abandon her. Obviously this is not brilliant, but it's stable.
I think I'll accept the proposition you so kindly made, of the position.

Mesa Are you sure?

De Ciz Sure.

Mesa I'll see to it then. I think you've made the right choice.

De Ciz I hope so, it's not what I dreamed of.

MESA	I know, you're a poet and you're a visionary. But you have a family to take care of. You need to see safety and benefit.
DE CIZ	That's what I hear all day.
MESA	I need someone now for the railroad. Courage, that's what I need, someone sensible with initiative. Someone like Amalric, do you have news of him?
DE CIZ	I think he's gone down to his plantation.
MESA	Such a man!
DE CIZ	He's a rogue and a brute.
MESA	You have other qualities, you're soft and refined. You'd have done well with the locals. That's why I thought of you.
DE CIZ	If I succeed at this mission, I'm a made man.
MESA	Let's not think about it anymore.
DE CIZ	Let me think about it a bit more.
MESA	No, Ciz, believe me. This country is bad, pirates, famine, illness I would not hesitate but I am not married. Madame De Ciz Urged me not to make you go. Although it's only a year or two.
DE CIZ	My wife has nothing to do with it. Mesa, I'm your man, I'll go.
MESA	Take more time to think about it.
DE CIZ	It's thought about, once I've made up my mind, that's it.

MESA   Then you're alone wanting it.
              Remember you'll be leaving against my opinion and
        my advice.

DE CIZ   I know that, Mesa. You're absolved.

MESA   As you wish. So be it.

DE CIZ   You're a friend to me.

MESA   A sincere friend.

DE CIZ   A good, sincere friend.

MESA   You won't find another such.

They exit.

ACT III

A port in Southern China at the moment of an insurrection. A house in the old colonial style. There are signs of a recent siege: huge sacks, windows blocked with mattresses. In the middle of the main room there is a large brass bed covered with a mosquito net. Between two windows, there is a dressing table with swing mirrors.

Ysé has her knitting on her lap as Amalric enters. She half turns toward him without looking at him and opens her arms to him. They embrace for a long while and when he tries to raise himself, she holds him back violently. He cries out.

AMALRIC	Ouch!
YSÉ	Did I hurt you my love?
AMALRIC	It's nothing. These old pop guns Have an absurd recoil, I've put my shoulder out. And I'm as dirty as a pig. I need a bath.
YSÉ	I love you.
AMALRIC	Look, the sun is setting Ysé.
YSÉ	So what? Let it set.
AMALRIC	He's off. Has business elsewhere, you see. We won't get it back, it's finished you see.
YSÉ	Very good sun. No denying it, he's done us proud, There isn't another. Look at him, There, like a great golden beast Who lays his head on your shoulder and you gently stroke it with your cheek. Goodbye my beautiful sun! We loved each other well you and I! Amalric, are we really going to die?
AMALRIC	I'm afraid so.
YSÉ	No tiny chance of escape?
AMALRIC	None. We're in a trap. They've been pretty good to us up 'til now. They like me actually. And I like them. They're not a bad lot these people. But now that the others have passed, It's too bad it's our turn. There's nothing left to say.
YSÉ	They won't take us alive.

AMALRIC	Have no fear my love.
YSÉ	Ah! I can still hear those cries When they stormed the club yesterday. How quickly it went up in flames. And that woman who jumped from the roof! It was horrible to see all those yellow bodies swarming together like a cake full of maggots.
AMALRIC	Oh you whitest of white women ! It's funny, I like them! You put them together and push. You could fill a boat with them, like bulk wheat, they're just flowing with no empty space between them! My recruitment was getting along famously but Adios! No more copra! No more rubber! Great idea of mine to come here at all.

He sighs.

YSÉ	You won't let them take me alive? Listen.

She seizes his wrist. Noise outside that little by little subsides.

Listen. Ta! Ta! Is that what they're shouting? Yes! Ta! Ta! Do you hear?

AMALRIC	It's nothing! There's no need to dig your nails into me. Just finishing off yesterday's business! Probably a missionary they're slicing in two. What was left of him.
YSÉ	They won't come here?
AMALRIC	I tell you, you have nothing to fear. We gave them too good a reception the other day. There's some strange ritual going on, my old lackey came to tell me about it yesterday.

                    Some day of the fox or pig.
                    Tomorrow! Tomorrow it'll be too late. No one left!
                    Finished! Tralala! The Yang Kwee-tse blown away!

Ysé   Have you done everything?

Amalric   Wonderful stuff this gelatine! You saw it the other day
                    when I set off my mine. I dare say it was a beautiful job.
                    It'll uproot this cantine like a miniature volcano.
                    Beautiful eh? Just right. Better than fizzling out on a
                    porcelain bedpan.
                    We won't die, we'll disappear in a clap of thunder!
                    Pell-mell, bodies and souls.
                    The dogs, the cats, we'll fart through the roof!
                    And the furniture. And the bastard along with us!

                    Ysé looks at him, terribly.

                    Oh! What a look! I love saying these things to you.
                    Something crosses your face like a flash from a canon-
                    shot you can't hear,
                    Because it's too far off. Don't get angry.

Ysé   I know that you love me.

Amalric   And that I love this child too?

Ysé   I know.

Amalric   As if I'd made him, I'm the only father he has. I took you
                    and him with you. You're mine and he's mine too and there's
                    the end of it.
                    When I saw you again on that second boat "oh no!" I
                    thought,
                    "No fooling around this time! Here she comes again,
                    right under your nose!"
                    "This is it." I never saw you look prettier.
                    You had no choice but to give in.
                    Yes, in spite of your tigresse looks you know I'm stronger,
                    it's written! I didn't ask your opinion.

This proud Ysé! With her hats and her peals of laughter and her queenly airs,

She was taken all the same, and here she is, submissive, tender, faithful,

Following this devil of a man who strides ahead, nose in the air!

And the husband, no more husband, and the children, what children? And the last lover,

Fruit you've had enough of, you wipe your mouth, there's just a little taste left, an after-taste, fingers into the finger-bowl where there's a piece of lemon.

YSÉ You know it's not true! You know I'm not so wicked, I love my children!

I thought I'd have them with me! You said I could fetch them!

AMALRIC Heaven! The things one says without knowing!

YSÉ And here I am with you, God knows how.

AMALRIC Poor Ysé! Wretched to be a woman.

He kisses her head.

Make some tea.

He looks out the window.

Nothing but rice. Field turning green and the river flaring.

See the tide of the night rising.

He sees her.

What is it, pigeon?

YSÉ Oh Amalric, you are hard! Oh God, God! It is hard!

AMALRIC		No tears, little one!
		What a good housewife you'd have made!

YSÉ		Wouldn't I my love? I was made to live a quiet and peaceful life
			Like other women. You see what a good wife I make.

AMALRIC		True, Ysé

YSÉ		It's good to know we're going to die after all, no one can enter and everything is closing in on us now.
			No one can hurt or abuse me now.
			Is it true, all I seem to have done? Was it I or someone else?
			My husband deceived, abandoned, my poor children,
			I left them, I don't even know where they are! And that miserable man I loved
			And who loved me more than life, I'd hardly left him than I betrayed him and gave myself to you
			With a child in my womb, as if driven by some urgent sense of duty.

AMALRIC		It must've stunned Mesa.

YSÉ		He knows everything now. Oh those dreadful letters before the port closed.
			I'm only a wretch of a woman. What do I know? What do they want from me? What could I do? All these people that cling to me, it's not my fault!
			That terrible woman! Well at least she's arranged to do no more harm to anyone.
			What I hunger and thirst for is no longer to live and for none to be left to despise me.

AMALRIC		Why should they despise you, I'd like to know?

YSÉ		You are good Amalric.
			I know I've done nothing wrong. When I think, when you explain it to me,

I see that I had to do what I did, things couldn't be otherwise.

And Mesa, yes, I did him a favour by leaving him. How did he find out where I was?

But oh Amalric however I try to reason, it's too much.

There are times when it's too much and too much and too much and enough, I can't take it anymore. I'm too alone, torn apart, too far away from everything I love.

And I'm too unhappy, too punished, and I pray to die, I'm afraid of dying, and I'm happy to die.

AMALRIC Is it as hard as that Ysé?

YSÉ No, it's not hard, my heart! No, it's not hard, my heart!
No, it's not hard with you. I regret nothing. I'm content.
Yes. It's all the same to me and what I did
I'd do again and I have no children, no friends
And I'm a horror to all, and I'm going to die, and I am content
That there is nothing but you alone for me, and me alone for you.

But it is horrible to be dead. (*She grows anxious and takes his hand*)

Amalric tell me the truth; Is it true, are we sure that it's true that there really is no God?

AMALRIC What would he do huh? If there was, I would have told you

YSÉ Good. There is none. So I have nothing to reproach myself with.

What I did I'd do again. It's the fault of the man I married.

And yet there are times where, you know, it's like when you feel there is someone watching you, looking at you,

There's no escape and whatever you do,

If you kiss me, if you laugh, he is a witness. He is watching us at this very moment.

And is that really worthy of you God? Does there have to be something so solemn and serious with a woman?

Patience, patience, one more little moment and we shan't be here.

AMALRIC   I recognize Mesa's language. These are absurd dreams.
Let your God look as much as he wants to, that's his affair. I say he's not.
I saved you from Mesa. You're not for him. You and I
Are creatures of reality. Reality not dreams. Reality, you understand? Reality, nothing else is true!

YSÉ   He has written me terrible letters. But he is unfair to me.
And this child of his which is mine, it's mine,
I carried him in my womb, what has that to do with a man?
And I want to live!
And I saw you on that boat, and I clung to you, and I thought you were life and that you would save me and that I could live with you,
Sanely, wisely, truthfully.

AMALRIC   Well, you can say that it's exactly how things turned out!

YSÉ   Everything worked out.
All that life that I could have given you, I die with you.
But him,
Why did he force me to go as soon as he knew I was pregnant? Should he have given me a moment?
Secretly, sneakily with all his soul he longed for me to go. Did he think I couldn't see it in his eyes? I had to go. I'd asked if he was happy and he looked at me with his air of a bad priest.

AMALRIC   He honestly loved you?

YSÉ   He loved me as you will never love me. And I loved him.
As I will never love you. Duty ties me to you because I am loyal and I know what I've done.
But with him it was despair and desire and a gust of wind, and a kind of hate, and flesh recoiling, and a thrust from my entrails like a child to draw out.

You conquered me but do not know what a woman unconquered is.

The desert and the thirst and the misery of love, and the fact of that other living, and that moment when you look into his eyes, and how it feels when the other soul is thrust into your own.

A year.

A year it lasted. I felt he was captive

But I did not own him and there was something foreign in him,

Impossible.

So how can he blame me? He didn't give himself and I withdrew.

And I, I wanted to live as well and to see again this earthly sun and live and live again

And live this life which is the life of everyone, and to escape all that love which is death.

And that's what happened. I accept everything.

AMALRIC   I love you Ysé.

YSÉ   Yes.

AMALRIC   I'll go do the round. We still have tonight which is ours.

A sound can be heard outside, then steps on the staircase. The door opens. Ysé does not turn her head. Mesa enters. He takes a few steps and then stands some distance from the chair where Ysé is seated. She remains motionless.

MESA   It's me.

Silence.

Mesa.

Silence.

All my letters over this past year.
Haven't you received all my letters over this past year?

Why didn't you answer them?

Nothing! Not a word! Not a single line! What did I do my darling, why make me suffer as you have?

What did I do to you? But in the end you are here and that's enough. It's you!

And I demand nothing, reproach you nothing. It's you, my soul! I see you! It's you and that's enough. I love you, Ysé!

Silence.

Yes, yes, it's true, I wanted you to leave! I was false in my heart and you knew it.

And I've seen what it is to be without you, you are my heart and my soul and my soul's lack, and I can't be without Ysé.

I don't believe what they told me. Not a word from you, cruel!

I don't believe what they said. And you're here. And you'll explain everything. Of course. Of course.

Forgive me for those last terrible letters, I was mad!

I don't believe you no longer love me! No, Ysé, I don't believe it! No, my heart! Just speak, my love. Turn to me, give me a word so that I hear and die of joy,

Because I lost you and I found you again!

Silence.

What did I do to you? Why do you treat me like this?

Not answering, as if I didn't exist.

If I were in the house with the dead I should recognize my only one, Ysé, Ysé! That's your name, Ysé. Don't you hear me? Ysé. What did I do to you? Heart of iron! Speak, tell me what you have against me? How have I suddenly deserved

This? What have I not given to you? Tell me! What I've kept back? Tell me so that I know!

My body, my soul,

My soul to do with what you liked, my soul as if it were mine, and you took it,

As if you knew what it was for.

If I made you go away, you know I had to.

You said so yourself,

But now I tell you Ciz is dead and I can take you for my wife.

We can love now without secrecy or remorse.

Don't you hear? Is it true, Ysé? You don't love me anymore? I received such a horrible letter!

No, Ysé, I don't believe it! No, my heart, I don't believe it!

And it doesn't matter and I want to forget it! Come, Ysé. And I'll save you, I shall take you back, and who can tear you from my heart?

Get up. Get up and I will save you Ysé, I will save you from Death because you see, I've come for you.

Silence.

Don't you believe me? I'm an old Chinaman and I know all the secrets.

I have a sign on me which everyone respects, as well as money.

Come, take your child, our child, he is our child after all!

Do you hear me? Is life such a tiny thing? Come.

It's life I'm bringing you.

Silence.

Come. I will save you. If you're finished with me
Let me at least take you back to your children.

Silence.

So, it's true! It's true!
So, so, that man.
You love him. And you don't love me, you hate me! You love him, you sleep with him.
And death, death with him,
You prefer over life with me!
And yet you did love me! When you left on the boat

I tried to kiss your cheek and it was you who, all tears,
Took my mouth violently with yours. Two weeks, only two weeks!

Silence.

Whore! What were your thoughts the first time
You bedded that stray dog?
Were my child's first stirrings merged with the ecstasies of a double adultery
And the life seed I gave you, when filled with the limbs of my ripening son, you slept in that other man's arms?
I beg you, I feel something in me trembling! Don't make me commit a greater crime, you don't know how close we are, you and I
To damnation at this moment. Just a breath away.

Silence.

The same woman.
Tell me, Ysé, this is no longer the great noon sun.
Remember our ocean? And later that boat which together we watched vanish away in the smoke.
Now the sepulchral lamp colours your cheek, and your ears, and your temple,
And your hair, the same hair ah I recognize that smell,
When I was plunged in you into a deep cavern, up to the nostrils.

Silence.

The sun has gone out.
The last great sun of our love, this great sun of Noon in August
Goodbye Ysé, you never knew me!
Couldn't root out
The greater treasure I have in me,
Couldn't take it, I didn't know how to give it. It's not my fault.

It is! It's our fault and our punishment. We had to give all,

I couldn't, and that's why you haven't forgiven me.

Silence.

And I have to endure this! She's not answering! She's here, O God, she's right here!

She's here and she's not here. The same, not the same.

Silence.

But you haven't the right! You haven't the right! It's not just you!

It's not true that you're forgotten me! It's not true you've stopped loving me! My love, It's not true you hate me!

There is no way, Ysé ! What I have given you, can I take it back? Don't you carry me with you where you go? Do you have the right

To not be mine? What is there within you that you haven't

Given me, that I haven't had, eaten, breathed in, feeding me with fire, tears and despair?

Answer me! See how I suffer. Turn your face towards me, my beauty, and tell me it's not true!

Silence.

Ysé, what have you done with my child?

Silence.

Is he dead?

Silence.

Ysé, you won't simply let him die? Give me my child to save.

Silence.

Is he dead? Have you killed him?

Silence.

If he's here, I shall find him.

Amalric's footsteps are heard. He enters.

AMALRIC   Who's there?

MESA   It's me.

AMALRIC   Mesa, I'm not at all happy to see you.

MESA   I've come to take back this woman who is mine and the child who is mine.

AMALRIC   You shall have neither.

MESA   I shall take them back regardless.

AMALRIC   And regardless of her perhaps? What do you say, Ysé?
What do you prefer? Speak.
To go with him and live,
You and the child, if so put out your hand.
Or to die with me?

Silence. Ysé remains motionless.

MESA   This is too much !

Mesa draws a weapon. Amalric throws himself on him and tears the weapon from him. There is a horrible fight in the darkness. Mesa collapses. Ysé who sees everything in the mirror, hasn't moved.

YSÉ   *In a strange voice and without changing position.*

Murderer!

Amalric lights a lamp and bends over and examines Mesa's body.

AMALRIC	Just as I thought. I've dislocated his right shoulder And it seems he's shattered a leg himself. What a clumsy fool!
	Strange, strange how you understand one another when you fight. Mesa and I have learned more about one another in a minute than in a whole lifetime together.
YSÉ	Amalric, this is hideous. Don't just leave him there lying on the ground.
	It's not right.
AMALRIC	How did he get as far as this?
YSÉ	He said he had a pass.

Amalric searches Mesa's pockets and finds a document covered with strange characters, which he shows to Ysé.

AMALRIC	Interesting. I suspect we are saved, Ysé.
YSÉ	Saved.
AMALRIC	How sadly you said that.
YSÉ	My husband is dead, we can be married, Amalric
AMALRIC	Marvellous. What more can I ask? An excellent evening. What a fine little Christian household we'll make!
YSÉ	Is there no way of taking him with us!
AMALRIC	Impossible
YSÉ	We can't just abandon him to the Chinese.
AMALRIC	He'll blow up in our place. The bomb is set, just let it tick.
YSÉ	*In the same strange voice.*

Empty his pockets, no need to leave anything to a dead man.

Amalric Ysé, it's a bit disgusting.

Ysé Why? Just do it.

Amalric pulls out a sealed envelope.

Amalric *Reading*
"This is my testament"

He laughs and puts the envelope in his pocket.

Get ready. I saw the boat coming in.
I will call my boy. Everything will be alright. Take the child.

Ysé exists, then comes back.

Ysé Let's leave.

Amalric You're not taking the child?

Ysé: He's dead.

Amalric Let's go

He blows out the lamp. They leave without looking at Mesa.
Pitch black. The stars can be seen. The moonlight shines in the room.
Mesa revives, but remains silent, meditating.

MESA'S CANTICLE

MESA Here I am in my funeral chapel!
And on all sides, left and right, I see a forest of torches around me!
No candles burning, but powerful stars, like blazing virgins
Facing God, as we see in sacred paintings, Saint Mary atoning!
And I, the human, the Intelligent being,
I'm lying on the earth, ready to die, on a solemn catafalque,
At the deepest point in the universe, at the very centre of this bubble of stars, of this hive, of this worship,
I see the huge clergy of the Night with its bishops and its patriarchs
And above me, the Pole and on my sides, the Equator, and the Milky Way!
Hail sisters! I'm alone! No priest with his pious community here
To give me absolution.

Why? I'm asking why this woman? Why suddenly, so cleverly, this woman on the boat
At the crucial moment? What has she got to do with us? Did we need her? It was you alone!
You didn't ask my opinion!
You took over!
You alone in me suddenly and all doors closed.
You gave the orders, what could I do? I tried! Crafty trick of yours to be stronger.
And crafty too to bring me this woman, one could say You chose her!
Forty days. To put me there for forty days, face to face with her on that boat, so that I had all that time to look at her, no pressure,
She whom it had to be.
Did I believe in her? For a single moment?
I said for a single moment, for one single moment did

I believe in her and that happiness laid in her arms?
  I was a captive grinding my teeth who couldn't move!
  It's crafty, all of a sudden to have put this woman forty days in front of me on the boat. She who it had to be.
  It's crafty to play the God with me all of a sudden!
  Because You've refused me and the other took me.
  And in a moment, I will see You and I'm frightened.
  Scared in the pith of my bones.
  And You will question me. And I will question You!
  Am I not a man? Why do You play God with me?
  No, No, no I'm not asking You anything.
  You're here. That's enough. Just listen.

  Because I loved You.
  As one loves gold because it's beautiful or a fruit you want to eat right away!
  No doubt that I did not love You as one should, rather for my own knowledge or my own pleasure.
  And I found myself before You as someone who realises how alone he is.
  And I got to know my own nothingness, and I got closer to my own flesh.
  I've sinned.
  Now, Save me, God, it's enough!
  Since I've been selfish, that is how You punish me
  With this horrible love for another!

  I know now
  What love is! And I know what You've endured on the cross, in your Heart,
  If You loved each of us
  Terribly, as I loved this woman.
  I loved her and she did that to me!
  I loved her and I'm not afraid of You.
  Above Love,
  There's nothing, not even You.
  And she did that to me!
  You know yourself what betrayed Love feels like! I'm not afraid of you!
  Let us die and leave this miserable body!

Let us leave, my soul, and break free from this detestable carcass.

Light, silky sound from outside. The door opens silently. Ysé, dressed in white, enters in a kind of trance. She moves forward across the room like a cloud. She passes before the mirror. She can be seen through the mosquito net. She goes into the dead child's room, leaving the door half opened. She can be heard crying strangely.

MESA *Calling softly.*

Ysé! Ysé!

She comes out and wanders soundlessly across the room. She opens the drawers of the chest, of the dressing table, and puts her hands into them. She opens the wardrobes, the medicine cabinet. She runs her fingers over the empty shelves, she raises herself up as if to look. She moves to the office, to the dining room, everywhere, like someone who is rummaging and searching for something, mistress of the deserted house.
Silence.

Suddenly a woman's loud cry is heard, frighteningly melodious and shrill.

MESA *Calling more forcefully.*

Ysé! Ysé! come! come!

Pause. Then suddenly Ysé is seen all white in the moonlight.

MESA Ah, just as a saw you on the boat!

She comes toward him and crouches at his feet. She places her bare arm straight across his knees. He gently places his hand on her head.

YSÉ Mesa, I am Ysé. It is I.

MESA Really you?
How often I've seen you in dream. Is this one more dream? Will you stop existing again?

Ysé	This is not a dream, Mesa, dreams are over. There is nothing now but truth.
Mesa	Ah, be my life, my Ysé, be my soul and my heart.
Ysé	Leave your hand on my head and then I can see and understand everything.
You don't really know who I am, but now I see clearly who you are and who you want to be
Full of light and glory, a creature of God! And I see that you love me
And that you are assigned to me, and I am with you in a wordless tranquillity.
Mesa	Is everything over, Ysé?
Ysé	Everything is over!
Mesa	Nothing more to fear?
Ysé	It's done.
Mesa	Nothing more to expect?
Ysé	Nothing but love forever, nothing but eternity with you!
Mesa	And so I can't get rid of this Ysé?
I can't take away these two hands on my sides?
Ysé	Impossible. Wherever you are, I am with you.
Mesa	Why did you leave me?

Pause

	Why won't you answer?
Ysé	Why did you push me away so desperately?

Mesa	I loved you too much, my life!
Ysé	I can no longer be taken from you. But let me say what I have to say. Keep your hand on my forehead so that I can remember. Oh, how full of night and pain I feel! But my whole weight is spread out across your body and you cannot escape me. Let me tell you everything. Let me speak to you in bitterness.
Mesa	Your golden head is there beneath my hand.
Ysé	Mesa, our child is dead.

She begins to sob softly.

Mesa	It is better that way.
Ysé	You never saw him, Mesa.
Mesa	I will see him in a moment and he will recognize me.
Ysé	Oh what bitterness! O child of my shame! Ô dearest child, child of my womb! Forgive your miserable mother! Ô Mesa, a child, you don't know what it means. How much you feel a woman with your child!
Mesa	Peace, Ysé!
Ysé	O Mesa, don't let me wake up. I don't want to. Don't let me become that old Ysé again, the proud, beautiful Madame Ciz.
Mesa	It's no longer the old Ysé, it's my Ysé with me now forever.
Ysé	I left him At the very moment the boat took off. He thought I was sleeping in the bedroom.

MESA   Why are you taking my hand so convulsively?

YSÉ   Don't leave me Mesa!
          I can see everything!
          I've done dreadful things!

MESA   What do you see?

YSÉ   A wretched straw hut, a dead man
          With a horrible face,
          Wracked with cholera, in a filthy blanket. No longer that insipid look I hated!
          From the roof a drop of water
          Falls ceaselessly on the pupil of his open eye.

MESA   What else do you see?

YSÉ   O my children!
          What kind of mother was I for you!
          How they would look at their dear mother with their trusting, peaceful eyes as I read to them.
          And I think of how I've betrayed and abandoned and murdered them!
          Sometimes at night if I woke up, I could hear them sleeping with their different breathing,
          And I would listen, my heart beating, and I would think, these are my dear children!
          You know there never were more beautiful children! They never gave me the slightest trouble.
          Everyone would look at us when we went out,
          I, the triumphant mother between her sons, and they walking beside me,
          Upright, clenching their fists like little soldiers.
          I don't understand! I'm just a wretched woman!
          How did all this happen?

MESA   It's *love* that made it happen. And isn't that still the only thing that is good and true and just and meaningful?
          Have words lost their meaning? Don't we still call *good* what facilitates

Our love, and *bad* what hinders it?
It's true that we haven't spared
Others. And what about us ? Have we spared ourselves?
Look at me here with my limbs torn apart like a criminal on the wheel,
And you, your soul outraged, coming out of your body like a sword half unsheathed.
But even evil contains some good that shouldn't be lost.
We cannot bring the dead back to life, but we still have our own death.
We can therefore turn our faces honestly toward the Avenger,
And say, "Here we are. Pay yourself what we owe."
That much we can do.

Pause.

And all sacraments gathered into one, I say that I consent to you, Ysé.

Ysé	I consent to you, Mesa.
Mesa	It is finished, my soul.
Ysé	Don't be afraid, Mesa.
Mesa	I'm not afraid, Ysé.
Ysé	Don't be ashamed, little Mesa, it's the one most full of life who dreads

No longer living the most. O how hard and closed men are, and how afraid they are of suffering and dying!
But the female, Woman, mother of man,
Isn't daunted, being familiar with the silent hands that pull.
I see your heart, Mesa, I'm satisfied.
I was jealous, Mesa, I saw you sombre, and I knew
You were hiding a part of yourself from me.
But now I see everything and all of me is seen, and there is nothing but love between us.

MESA   We didn't know how to give ourselves half-way, Ysé !
               Let's give ourselves altogether and all at once !
               And already I can feel inside me
               All the old powers of my being giving way to a new
         order.

Ysé rises and stands before Mesa, her eyes closed, white in the moonlight.

YSÉ   Now look at my face for there is still time
               And see me standing upright and spreading out like a
         great olive tree in the earthly moonlight,
               Take stock of this mortal face for the time of our
         resolution draws near
               and you will no longer see me with your bodily eye !
               And I hear you and I don't hear you for already I no
         longer have ears to hear !
               Don't be silent, beloved, you are there!
               Only give me your consent so that
               I may spring forth
               Like a true voice to your voice, your eternal Ysé!
               I was beneath you, body yielding, and like a horse
         between your knees who goes where you turn its head, a
         wild horse who goes further and faster than you want!
               See her unfurling now, O Mesa, the woman full of
         beauty opening into the even greater beauty!
               Rise up, broken form, and see me as a dancer,
         listening,
               Whose tiny jubilant feet are gathered up by the
         irresistible measure!
               Follow me, don't delay!
               Here I am laughing, rolling, uprooted, my back on the
         very substance of the light.
               O Mesa, this is the break at midnight! And here I am
         ready to be set free,
               The sign for the last time of this mass of hair unleashed
         in the wind of Death!

MESA   Farewell! I have seen you for the last time!
               On what long, painful, still distant paths,

Always weighing on one another,
Will we lead forth
Our labouring souls?
Remember, remember the sign !
And mine is not vain hair in the wind and the little handkerchief for a moment,
But all veils cast aside, myself, the great flashing flame in the glory of God,
Man in the splendor of August, Victorious Spirit in the transfiguration of Noon!

Paul Claudel

Based largely on the 1906 version.
Translations by Jonathan Griffin 1970,
Susannah York 1991, David Furlong 2018,
John Naughton 2021.

Alternate ending based on the 1949 version, and beginning after Mesa's canticle:

In this version, after Amalric has wounded Mesa, he places him in a large Chinese chair with a circular back in the form of an Omega. It is in this chair that Ysé finds him when she returns.

A light silky sound from outside. The door is opened silently. Ysé enters in a kind of trance, moving forward across the room like a cloud. She passes in front of the mirror. She can be seen through the mosquito net. She stops motionless and upright behind Mesa's chair.

MESA   Ysé, Ysé, come! Come!
Ah, just as I saw you on the boat!

YSÉ   Mesa, I am Ysé. It is I.

She crouches at his feet and places her naked arm right across his knees. He gently places his hand on her head.

MESA   Is it?
I have been dreaming of you so often! Is this another dream? Will you stop existing again?

YSÉ   It's no dream, Mesa. Dreams are over.
There's only truth.

MESA   Tell me, do you hear me now? Do you feel
My breathing in your entrails? Be my life, Ysé, be my soul, and in my arms, and in my heart.
Ysé, don't be so cruel, don't push me away, I am the one in your heart.

YSÉ   You don't know who I am but I see clearly now who you are and who you want to be.
Filled with light and glory, a creature of God! And I see how you love me,
And you're assigned to me and I'm with you now.

MESA   Is it all over, Ysé?

YSÉ   Over.

MESA   Nothing to fear?

YSÉ   Nothing.

MESA   No more, nothing to expect?

YSÉ   Nothing more than love forever, nothing else than eternity with you!

MESA   I can't get rid of this Ysé?

YSÉ   Impossible. Where you are, I am too.

MESA   Why did you leave me?
          I'm listening. Everything that's in your heart, I'm here to listen to.

YSÉ   Do I have the right to take your hand?

MESA   Take it.

YSÉ   Not the right hand, the left. The one that hurts you. That's the one I love best. The left hand. You have the right to tell the left hand everything.

MESA   It would be even better if you were closer.

YSÉ   You mean there is room next to you in this big round chair?

MESA   There's room. It's not like the rocking chair. You can come next to me if you want.

YSÉ   Really? Monsieur is willing to have me join him on this chair?

MESA		Come.

YSÉ		The jaws have closed on us again. We are taken and there is no way of escaping.

Ysé seats herself close to Mesa. There is moonlight that little by little comes to the chair, then eventually passes on.

YSÉ:		It's best to be together for what is going to happen.
		Both together. This is what I've come to bring to you. There is no need for explanation. My heart. My heart with yours so that you feel it. Can you hear? *(Softly)* It's beating! My heart is what I've come to bring to
			You.
		This flesh, Mesa, which grows warm against yours.

MESA:		I recognize it only too well.

YSÉ:		It's funny. One thing is sure! Sure! We were made to be together, the two of us. There is that.

MESA:		Yes.

YSÉ		There is that. But do you know something else, my little Mesa, and it's why I've come to bother you.
		There was no way I could let you leave like that without you knowing it, Yes, I absolutely had to tell you. Are you listening carefully? You feel how nice it is for her to be with you right now, your Ysé?

MESA:		I'm listening.

YSÉ		Tell me, my little Mesa, did you know how much I hated you?"

MESA:		I knew.

YSÉ:		I had a peaceful life after all.
		And that Ysé didn't want to die any more than anyone else.

I was young, beautiful!

And my children! I've betrayed them and abandoned them and murdered them!

But it happened. You happened. There was no way out. I knew there was no way out.

I tried, it's not my fault. You can't say I didn't try. There was no way out.

MESA   It's true.

YSÉ   I tried. You have nothing to reproach me for!

MESA   No.

YSÉ   And you, sometimes, I know, ah how you hated me. You think I couldn't see it in your eyes, what you had in your eyes! That hatred all at once, that terrible desire, that desperate desire, to have me go away, at any cost, in any way, and that I tear myself from you! This is what gave me that sort of despair.

I tried! You, you would never have been able to. What do you have to blame me for? Ah, that priestly look that pierced me like a red-hot iron! And I, too, at those moments, did you know how much I hated you?

Softly, tenderly, she snuggles close to him.

MESA: Yes, I knew.

YSÉ   See, Mesa, our two hearts, these two hearts, tell me, can you feel it, these two hearts, my heart against yours, my flesh against yours, we are going to die, we're warm together we two, these two hearts, Mesa, it's funny the way they can detest each other!

All the things we have to forgive one another!

And this Ysé you're not going to be able to get rid of her so easily. She's hitched to you, the filthy beast!

MESA   I accept. I consent. I am paying. I have paid.

YSÉ Dearly!

MESA Dearly.

YSÉ Dearly! And that's what you don't like, my little Mesa, paying dearly!
    One pretends to give everything, but deep down, one's quite determined to keep it all for oneself. That's how you must have offered yourself to God, little Mesa, something so tight, so closed that I would have loved to have seen how the good lord would have figured out how to open it without breaking his nails!
    It's not good, my little Mesa, to be stingy. It's ugly to be the damn self-centred egotist you were!

MESA What the good lord couldn't get from me, you certainly succeeded in getting.

YSÉ Is it true that I succeeded? Is it true that I taught you what it means to belong to another? Is it true that I really taught you what it means to have someone tear you from your very shoes? The marrow, my little Mesa, the soul as they say, the root, that was what I was after. Someone was needed for that!
    Woman, after all, the good lord made her, so she should have some use after all, the filthy beast! You only asked me for my body, but for me, it was something else I was after, something else!
    When one has taken everything from a woman, she should be given something back in its place.

Pause.

    All the same, Mesa, the world, for however vast it is, there is one thing it couldn't give you.

MESA What thing?

YSÉ Your true name. That true name that is yours and that I alone know.

>   My soul that is your name, my soul that is your key,
> my soul that is your cause. That name that is yours, your
> name that is inseparable from me.
>   And that you would have to tear from me.

MESA   And now there is death.

YSÉ   How intelligent he is, this little Mesa! He has
understood. Yes, little fellow, there is death. And it is from
my hand alone that you could receive it.

She straightens herself slowly and raises her arm and then her hand.

>   The stars in the sky Mesa.
>   You've seen them haven't you?
>   Someone was needed to give them to me.

MESA   I can't take them down for you.

YSÉ   It's easy. You have only to stretch out your hand.

She takes his hand and forces him up. She raises her hand with his gently and carefully as though the task were difficult. He rises with difficulty and stands upright.

>   Mesa, I am Ysé, It is I.
>   Look carefully at this mortal face for you will not see
> me again with your earthly eye,
>   But give me your consent so that I may spring forth
>   Like a true voice to your voice, your eternal Ysé.
>   I was beneath you, body yielding, and like a horse
> between your knees who goes where you turn its head, a
> wild horse that goes further and faster than you want
>   See her unfurling now, Mesa, the woman full of beauty
> opening into the even greater beauty

> *Ysé begins to disappear into the darkness.*

Here I am ready to be set free, my face is disappearing into night
Remember, Remember the one in the darkness for a moment who was
Your eternal Ysé.

Pause. Silence. Only Mesa's luminous, raised hand is seen, as the curtain falls abruptly.

END

Paul Claudel, 20th January 1949
Translation John Naughton, March 2021

Afterword

Susannah York

For Jonathan, without whom

Jonathan as long as I knew him bore a shining countenance; I'm sure he always did, for in that aged face nothing was more discernible than the small boy, merry, kind, naughty, bursting with secrets and questions and life.

I'd discovered Claudel's *Partage de midi* and determined I must play Ysé. No, no-one knew of an English version. I began to make heavy weather of the first pages of a first attempt, but then, yes! I heard from Tony Rudolf: the poet Jonathan Griffin had translated it some years ago, Ben Kingsley had played Mesa, there'd been a *succès d'estime* at Ipswich...

By the time I first met Jonathan, I'd discovered and read Claudel's two later versions of the play. The original – from which my enthusiasm had stemmed – was more poem than play, a glorious metaphysical piece rich in characterisation and *vie intérieure* but untheatrical; and Jonathan's translation of that 1905 version had those same qualities, but lacked the vocal rhythms of the French. On better acquaintance it was clear to me why Barrault, whilst twisting Claudel's arm in the early forties for the rights to the play, had insisted on extensive rewriting. Claudel himself wanted them in this his most personal work, and the first 'version pour la scène' contained much new material to make it stageworthy, even coarse in its theatricality. Evidently Claudel and Barrault soon thought so too, for when the play was revived some five years later, there was a newly cut and reshaped second *version pour la scène*, but to my mind (and Jonathan's too, when he read them), some of the fineness of the original was gone.

Jonathan Griffin: was he sage or elf? Both of course, but sage is what I knew of that first meeting, sage, poet, diplomat, linguist: and those are the ones I asked, not very hopefully, if they would consider working with me from scratch on not just a new translation, but a new version. 'Structure comes naturally to actors,' David Hare told me once: I felt essential to the reassembly. There's nothing like a plethora of indifferent scripts, either, for teaching you sayability... I felt essential to the translation too. Perhaps between us, headlong actor, faithful poet, we could, whilst being true to

Claudel, muster the inspiration needed to bring this very French piece to the English stage? To my everlasting enchantment Jonathan agreed.

I never found out whether he had collaborated in this way before, it seemed we were making up the way to work; at any rate I hadn't, and should it happen again I know I can't expect such joy. For three glorious summer months on and off we worked. At each day's end we'd repair with our *devoir*, the next pages to be individually prepared, and three or four mornings a week I would dash over to Primrose Hill (the sun seemed always to be shining), listen for the shuffling of Jonathan's sandals on the parquet. Spectacles skew-whiff, pencil 'twixt ear and finger, this etiolated pixie would sit me down at the dining-room table where he'd already been working and together we'd prise out, tease out, extract meaning, bend into English rhythms this dense and wondrous prose. He'd have no truck from me over our disparity in age, experience, status, exacting no quarter and giving none: and while again and again we'd agree on the happiest rendering of a word, a thought, a passage, just as often we didn't, Jonathan always fighting for the most exact translation, I for what, tried out on my tongue, could be said. Remarkable powers of persuasion would swing into play…

Golden hours. We worked joyfully, relentlessly, gasping for air after three or four hours, gulping down Kate's sandwiches sometimes, but mostly repairing to the pub where sitting in a stained-glass glow, we'd devour fish and chips or huge cheese-and-tomato rolls, as well as a good glassful each of wine as golden as stained glass; talk the play, talk Claudel, Jonathan's diplomatic work in Paris, an opera he'd just seen, the jobs I was between, Aldeburgh, politics, Jesuitry, poetry, theatre, family, life … and rush back to work at the dining-room table until the preparing sounds of Kate and our stomachs and the disappearing sunlight told us it was teatime and after. And one day we finished. Apparently we'd finished.

Laid down our pencils by the sheaves of paper scribbled and rescribbled over, on the dining-room table, and tiptoed away for tea, our last tea, Kate pouring, and those wonderful macaroons from Marks and Spencer and the chocolate cake: solemnly, sadly, chortling with achievement amongst the portraits in the sitting-room while the outrageously fat tabby purred. We knew it wasn't the end though; I was to take home the wads of paper, type them up, and next week we'd have a grand reading in my sitting-room. A grand reading of two. I'd read, Jonathan would listen. And after that the National and the RSC and Jonathan Miller at the Old Vic, the English-speaking world would be fighting for a chance to mount it, Kingsley and McKellen and Holm to play Mesa, Blakely and Jacobi and Gambon, Amalric…

But that's not what happened. Reading it aloud days later, I tripped and stumbled frequently, unaccustomedly; and realised in some despair that we were still very far from a final draft, though Jonathan professed himself pleased. The differences of our viewpoints sprang (perhaps?) from the fact that he 'saw' the text on the page, approved its literary authenticity: I said it, kept saying it, large chunks, and imaginatively hearing it both in my mouth and others' … and what so often looked real and true hardly sounded so, Claudel's passion dressed in English weights…

I put it away.

Over a year later I was touring in *The Glass Menagerie*. Once you feel you have your character and her story in the bone – and three weeks after opening I felt that with Amanda – you suddenly feel released, stimulated in fact to take on others, another, their story. I reread our translation. It didn't feel performable.

Starting again from scratch from the three French versions, with my so much augmented knowledge and understanding, was hardly even a decision. I left the translation in London, and easily unlearning the adopted metre in Swansea and Buxton and Norwich did just that for two or three pages, five or six… Three and a half weeks later the revised text and a new translation were done. It was a very different thing.

For weeks, for months I procrastinated about ringing Jonathan. Would he feel hurt, offended, used? How would he feel about his name there? How did I?

Eventually I rang him, and sent it, and waited…

He was speedy, and absolutely grand of course. 'Well, you've taken my breath away. It's marvellous. It's hardly the same thing. Marvellous though. All the same…' Winded, he sounded, but giggling and full of the same glorious enthusiasm for the play, and no, there'd been no travesty. 'But if I might make one or two observations…' and of course he was wonderfully pertinent over a Kate tea.

Later, through Tony, I learned that delicacy forbade him to suggest his name be taken off the translation, lest I suspect some private reservations. But were the suggestion to come from me…

When it is played it will be dedicated 'To Jonathan without whom.'

Anthony Rudolf: Post-Script

Susannah York's translation of *Partage de midi*, *Noonbreak*, was presented at the French Institute in London from November 19 till December 8, 1991 and then in the Green Room at the Manchester Royal Exchange Theatre. It was directed by Eloi Recoing, with Susannah York as Ysé, Michael Thomas as Mesa, Tim Woodward and Sam Cox as Amalric and De Ciz. Susannah York adds: 'When Eloi first demonstrated to me in speech the Claudelian verset – Claudel's completely original form of free verse inspired by his reading of the Psalms – as a way in which a phrase or a thought could be spoken in a single breath, I suddenly understood how the verse could set the actor on a wonderful roller-coaster... how, indeed, the text was thereby *underpinned*. With very little change of wording I re-cast my version into an English equivalent and it stood us in marvellous stead'.

Biographical Notes

Paul Claudel (1868–1955) was a French poet, dramatist and diplomat, and the younger brother of the sculptor Camille Claudel. A devout Catholic, he was best-known for his verse dramas. He was born into a family of farmers and government officials in the Aisne département. His father was a local government official, a registrar of mortgages, while his mother came from a family of farmers and priests. An unbeliever in his teenage years, Paul experienced a sudden conversion at the age of eighteen on Christmas Day 1886 while listening to a choir sing Vespers at Notre Dame de Paris. He would remain a devout Catholic for the remainder of his life.

As a young man, Claudel took up a post in the French diplomatic corps, in which he would serve for over 40 years – until his retirement in 1935 – although he underwent a period of doubt in the early years, when he seriously thought that he might have a monastic vocation. He was first vice-consul in New York, and then in Boston; French consul in various cities in China (1895–1909); then consul in Prague, Frankfurt, Hamburg, and Rome. He was Minister Plenipotentiary in Rio de Janeiro, and then Copenhagen; ambassador in Tokyo (1922–1926), Washington, D.C. (1927–1933) and Brussels (1933–1935), after which he retired.

Due to his position in the diplomatic corps, during the early part of his career Claudel published either anonymously or under a pseudonym. This led to him remaining obscure until the editors of the *Nouvelle Revue Française* recognised his work and began working with him.

The best-known of his plays are *Partage de midi* (1906), *L'annonce faite à Marie* (1911), and *Le soulier de satin* (1924). He also wrote the text for *Jeanne d'Arc au bûcher* (1934), Honegger's opera-oratorio. In addition to his verse dramas, Claudel also wrote a substantial corpus of lyric poetry.

Julia Farrer was born in London and studied at the Slade School of Art from 1968 to 1972 before teaching there until 1974, when she went to the United States on a Harkness Scholarship for two years. Farrer was based in Paris throughout 1978 and 1979 then returned to London to teach at the Wimbledon School of Art and at the Byam Shaw School of Art.

She produces geometrical abstract paintings and drawings, characterised by the use of distinct lines and pastel shades, that reflect rhythms found in nature. Her work has been included in a number of significant group shows and she has also had a number of solo exhibitions. Group shows that have featured her work include the first Nuremberg Drawing Biennial in 1979, the 1988 show *Composition/Structure* at the Galerie Lüpke in Frankfurt and the Harkness Artists '58-'85 retrospective at the Air Gallery in London. Solo exhibitions of Farrer's work have been hosted at The Air Gallery, Huddersfield City Art Galleries, Eagle Gallery and the JPL Gallery, and at the Francis Graham-Dixon Gallery in London. Farrer has also exhibited at Foire International d'Art Contemporain in Paris. A number of public collections hold works by Farrer including the Ashmolean Museum, Oxford, Metropolitan Museum of Art, New York, Tate Gallery, London, The British Museum, The British Library, Bibliothèque nationale de France, Paris, Fondation Rothschild, and Pfalzgalerie, Kaiserslautern.

DAVID FURLONG is a Mauritian actor, director, translator and deviser, who is bilingual in English and French. He trained at the National Theatre of Chaillot in Paris and he established his company, Exchange Theatre in London, in 2006, and has been its artistic director since then. The company co-founded with Fanny Dulin, makes French classical plays accessible to an English audience through translation and adaptation, as well as devised works around multilingualism. Recent productions include *The Flies* (Bunker Theatre), *The Misanthrope* (CPT/Drayton Theatre) and *The Doctor in Spite of Himself* (Drayton Theatre/French Lycee). David was also invited to direct and devise a dozen family productions for the French Institute in London over a period of 2 years. He was the Jerwood Assistant Director at the Young Vic in 2020 and received the SDUK Mentorship in 2017. David's work has been presented at The Finborough Theatre, The Bunker Theatre, The French Institute in London and Hackney Empire and he was a guest observer at the Royal Opera House (*Madama Butterfly*) and the National Theatre (*Hadestown*). David has also participated regularly in the Young Vic Genesis programme and has taught at Arts Educational as well as working on a number of community and school projects.

JONATHAN GRIFFIN (1906–1990) was Director of BBC European Intelligence during World War II. For the first few years after the war, he was responsible for cultural and educational matters at the British Embassy in Paris.

He resigned from the Foreign Office in 1951 and thereafter devoted himself to writing poetry and plays, subsidising his literary activities by translating prose books from the French. These translations included the first volume of General de Gaulle's memoirs, the memoirs of Jean-Louis Barrault, the plays of Henri de Montherlant, novels by Jean Giono and Romain Gary, art criticism by Dora Vallier and René Huyghe, and the cinematographic notebooks of Robert Bresson.

Griffin's long and complex verse play, *The Hidden King*, was performed at the Edinburgh Festival in 1957. Despite poor reviews it was a popular success but, like other practitioners of poetic drama, he went out of fashion with the onset of "kitchen sink" theatre. Between 1957 and 1983, he published seven books of poetry. He lived long enough to see his *Collected Poems* published in the U.S.A. in two volumes (1989 and 1990). Admired as a poet by Ted Hughes and others, Jonathan Griffin is probably best known as a distinguished translator of poetry and plays, mainly from the French, Portuguese and German. The plays include Kleist's *The Prince of Homburg* as well as Claudel's *Break of Noon*. His main poetry translations were of Fernando Pessoa (several volumes, including the Penguin Modern European Poets edition of Pessoa), Camões and René Char.

JOHN NAUGHTON is Harrington and Shirley Drake Professor of the Humanities in the Department of Romance Languages at Colgate University in New York. He has authored or edited eight books, among them *The Poetics of Yves Bonnefoy*, *Shakespeare and the French Poet*, and *Une intention de salut*. He has also written more than 50 articles, translations, and reviews in the area of modern French poetry and poetics. He is the recipient of the medal of the Collège de France, and in 2019, he was made a knight in the French Order of Arts and Letters.

ANTHONY RUDOLF's translations include books of poetry by Yves Bonnefoy, Edmond Jabès, Claude Vigée and the Russian poet Evgeny Vinokurov, and prose works by Balzac and Jean Clair. Recent books of his own include *Jerzyk*, an annotated edition of the diary of his cousin, the youngest recorded suicide of the Holocaust. Rudolf's collected poems, *European Hours*, was published in 2017. Rudolf is co-editor of the two-volume anthology of prose and poetry by Yves Bonnefoy. He was visiting lecturer at London Metropolitan University and Royal Literary Fund Fellow at the Universities of Hertfordshire and Westminster. He is FRSL and Chevalier de l'Ordre des Arts et des Lettres. 2021 sees the publication of his memoir, *Journey Around My Flat*, his novella *Pedraterra* and a short book on Isaac Rosenberg, *The Binding of Isaac*. He is preparing a critical edition of the little known translations by Ted Hughes of Yves Bonnefoy's *Théâtre de Douve*.

SUSANNAH YORK (1939–2011) was a movie star and, later, a stage actress of range and distinction. Her best films include *The Greengage Summer* and *They Shoot Horses, Don't They?* On stage, she starred in *A Streetcar Named Desire* and *The Glass Menagerie* by Tennessee Williams, and Shaw's *The Applecart*. She performed Cocteau's monologue *La voix humaine* in French and English, and played Ysé in *Break of Noon*. On the fringe, in pub theatres and venues like Jermyn Street Theatre, she directed and acted in many contemporary and classical plays, and compiled and performed a one-woman show: *Shakespeare's Women*. She was also a political activist; in particular, she felt strongly about the nuclear situation, and was a champion of Mordecai Vanunu. She wrote two books for children, *In Search of Unicorns* (1973) and *Lark's Castle* (1976).

www.ingramcontent.com/pod-product-compliance
Lightning Source LLC
Chambersburg PA
CBHW031350160426
43196CB00007B/798